The Life of General Stonewall Jackson

Mary L. Williamson

Christian Liberty Press

Arlington Heights, Illinois

Christian Liberty Press
502 West Euclid Avenue
Arlington Heights, Illinois 60004
www.christianlibertypress.com

Second Revised Edition
Revised by Michael J. McHugh and Edward J. Shewan
Layout and editing by Edward J. Shewan
Cover design and graphics by Eric D. Bristley

ISBN 1-930092-21-0

Set in Garamond and Tiffany

Printed in the United States of America

Acknowledgment

Special thanks are extended to Mr. James L. Marks for granting
us permission to utilize the images of Thomas J. Jackson located
on the cover of this book and Robert E. Lee located in the body
of the book. Information on these paintings by Hong Min Zou
is available from Mr. Marks' gallery. You may write to:

**The Marks Collection
1590 North Roberts Road
Kennesaw, GA 30144**

Preface

It is the publisher's firm belief that the people of America today need to be exposed to the lives of great and good American patriots who were followers of Jesus Christ. The life of General Thomas J. Jackson is worthy of just such attention, for it helps to remind us that truly great Americans are those who seek to remain loyal to God and to the U.S. Constitution.

In this brief sketch of the famous Civil War general, Thomas "Stonewall" Jackson, Mary L. Williamson has attempted to portray the wonder of his matchless military genius, his uprightness of conduct, his firm belief in an overruling Providence, and his unfailing submission to the divine will of the Lord Jesus Christ. These traits of character formed the cornerstone upon which Christ erected the edifice of his greatness, and upon which young people of our day would do well to build.

In preparing this work, the author carefully studied the classic reference work, written by Professor R. L. Dabney, on the life of General Thomas Jackson. Professor Dabney was Jackson's chief-of-staff during the War Between the States and had firsthand knowledge of Stonewall Jackson's personal character and military exploits.

This book is respectfully presented to the public in the hope that it will bless the lives of all who read it.

Michael J. McHugh
Arlington Heights, Illinois

The Confederate Memorial at Stone Mountain Park,
near Atlanta, Georgia

Contents

General Thomas J. "Stonewall" Jackson and His Officers

Chapter 1

An Orphan Boy

1824–1841

Thomas Jonathan "Stonewall" Jackson was born on January 21, 1824, at Clarksburg in western Virginia. His family came from Scotch-Irish stock. His great-grandfather, John Jackson, was born in Ireland but his parents moved to London

Birthplace of Thomas Jonathan Jackson Clarksburg, Virginia

when John was only two years old. John Jackson grew to be a great businessman. In 1748 he came to the New World to make his fortune and landed in the State of Maryland. A short time later, John Jackson married Elizabeth Cummins.

John Jackson soon moved West with his wife and eventually bought lands in what is now known as Upshur County, West Virginia. Since land was cheap then, he soon owned a large piece of land and became a rich man for those times. He was greatly aided by his brave wife Elizabeth. In those days the Indians still made war upon the settlers. It is said that in more than one of those Indian raids Elizabeth Jackson aided in driving off the Indian warriors. This good woman was noted for her fine mind, good looks, and great height.

When the great War for Independence started, John Jackson and several of his sons marched off to war and at its close came back safe to their Virginia home. In these lovely and fertile valleys, John Jackson and his wife Elizabeth passed long and active lives. The husband lived to be eighty-six years old while his wife lived to the great age of one hundred and five years. Her God-given strength of body and mind fitted her to rear a race of mighty men. Thomas Jackson was the great-grandson of these good people.

The father of Thomas Jackson was a good and kind man named Jonathan Jackson. This gentleman worked as a lawyer in the State of Virginia. He is said to have been a hardworking and godly man. Thomas's mother was Julia Neale, the daughter of a merchant in the village of Parkersburg on the Ohio River. Mrs. Jackson was a loving mother and devout Christian. Thomas had one brother, Warren, and two sisters, Elizabeth and Laura Ann.

Father of "Stonewall" Jackson

Shortly before Laura Ann was born, her sister Elizabeth became sick with a fever and died. Her father, worn out by care and misery, was also taken ill and, two weeks after her death, he was laid in a grave by her side. The dual loss of her husband and daughter undoubtedly caused Mrs. Jackson to prematurely give birth to Laura Ann on March 27, 1826.

After the death of Jonathan Jackson, it was found that he had not left any property for his widow and children. They were now without a home, so a private charity decided to give the widow a small house. Here she sewed and taught school, caring as well as she could for her little fatherless children.

In the year 1830, Julia married Mr. Woodson, a lawyer, who was pleased with her youth and beauty. Her children—Warren, Thomas, and Laura Ann—were now claimed by their father's family because they did not approve of the new marriage. As her new husband was not a rich man and her health was failing, she was eventually forced to give them up. Six-year-old Thomas and little Laura Ann, then only four years of age, were sent away to their grandmother Mrs. Edward Jackson, who lived at Jackson Mills. Warren had to be sent off to his Uncle Alfred Neale in faraway Parkersburg on the Ohio River.

After living at their grandmother's for only a few months, Thomas and Laura Ann were summoned to visit their mother who was desperately ill. She had become ill after she gave birth to a son named Wirt Woodson and, with little time left, she wanted to see her children. Death for her had no sting and Thomas said, many years later, that her dying words and prayers had never been erased from his heart. In the latter part of 1831, she was laid to rest not far from the famous Hawk's Nest on New River, West Virginia.

Thomas and Laura Ann were once again sent to Jackson Mills to live with their grandmother Jackson in Lewis county. They were happy there and came to know something of a real home. Their Uncle Cummins and Aunts Rebecca and Polly also lived there and grew fond of the children; they and grandmother Jackson took good care of Thomas and Laura Ann. Across the brook from the house was a large grove of sugar maple trees where the children would go to play "making sugar." It was a great pleasure for Thomas to build bridges for his little sister to walk on in crossing the brook; and many were the delights of the cool and fragrant forest.

As it turned out, their good life came to an end when their grandmother died in August of 1835. Since their aunts had married and moved on, their were no women left to raise the children. Laura Ann was sent to Aunt Rebecca White who lived near Parkersburg and Thomas was sent to live with Aunt Polly and her stern husband, Mr. Isaac Brake, near Clarksburg. Though Thomas could not live with his sister Laura Ann, he always cherished the warmest love for her. The very first money he ever earned was spent in buying Laura Ann a pretty silk dress.

Young Thomas was a handsome child with rosy cheeks, wavy brown hair, and deep blue eyes. It is said of him that, as a child, he was strangely quiet and manly. The sadness of his young life made him grow up very fast. When he was only eleven years old, he went one day to the home of his father's cousin, Judge John G. Jackson, in Clarksburg.

While eating his dinner, he said to Mrs. Jackson in a quiet way, "Uncle and I don't agree. I have quit him and shall not go back any more." This kind cousin tried to show him that he was in fault and that he should go back to his Uncle Brake. He only shook his head and said more firmly than ever, "No, uncle and I don't agree. I have quit him and shall not go back any more." It seems that his uncle had tried to govern him by excessive force instead of through his sense of right and wrong. This strange child calmly made up his mind not to stay where there would be constant warfare.

From Judge Jackson's residence he went that evening to the home of another cousin who also tried to persuade him to return to his Uncle Brake. Thomas only said, "I have quit there. I shall not go back there any more." The next morning he traveled alone on foot for eighteen miles until he came to the home of his Uncle Cummins Jackson, the half brother of his father.

There he soon felt quite at home again with his kind uncle. Uncle Cummins was a bachelor who owned a fine farm and mills. He was quite fond of his little nephew and took time to teach Thomas all the arts of country life. He treated him more as an equal than as a child, for he saw immediately the decent nature which he had to deal with.

In the fall of 1836, his brother Warren came to Jackson Mills to visit Thomas. Warren, who was now fifteen years old, had opened a school in Upshur County and had become a young man of learning. Thomas greatly admired him and was eager to go with him to visit Laura Ann who now lived at the home of Uncle Alfred on the Ohio River. When the brothers arrived at Uncle Alfred's, they had a joyous reunion with their beloved sister.

At that time, they heard of many people who were making a great deal of money by cutting wood on the river islands of the Ohio and Mississippi and selling it to passing steamboats. Warren eventually induced Thomas to leave their uncle's home to seek their fortunes in the great western part of the country. From Parkersburg they rafted downstream and no one heard from them for several months. In February of the following year, they returned to their kind relatives, ragged and ill with chills and fever.

Warren and Thomas on the Ohio River

Their story was that they made a raft and floated down to one of the lonely islands in the Mississippi River near the Kentucky shore where they cut wood for steamboats on the river. Here they spent the winter alone with little food, in the midst of a dense forest surrounded by the rushing waters of the great Mississippi. Eventually, illness forced them to seek their way home. Warren and Thomas stopped at the home of their Uncle Brake but Thomas boldly said that he was going back to his good Uncle Cummins. As a result of this experience, however, disease had laid so firm a hold upon Warren that, after lingering a few years, he died at the age of nineteen.

Thomas began to take private lessons from a neighbor Mr. Robert P. Ray; later, he went to a country school a little distance away at a place called McCann's Run. As a student, he showed no aptness for any study except arithmetic. When called upon to recite a lesson, Thomas would flatly say that he did not understand it and therefore was not ready; nor would he go to the next lesson until he had learned the first perfectly. Thus he was always behind his class.

He was never bad-tempered at school but was always ready for a fun game. When there were games of "bat and ball" or "prisoner's base," he was sure to be chosen captain of one side and that side generally won. Futhermore, if he was treated fairly by his playmates, he was gentle and yielding; however, if he thought himself wronged, he did not hesitate to fight it out. It is said that he would never admit that he had been beaten in a fight and was always ready to renew the contest when his foe challenged him again.

In the summer, Thomas worked on the farm and became of use to his uncle in many ways. One of his most frequent jobs was to haul great logs of oak and pine from the woods to the sawmill. He became a respected driver of oxen and was known throughout the countryside as a young man of great strength and courage. From the ages of nine to sixteen, his life passed between the school and the farm. He was then like his father, low of stature, but afterwards he grew tall.

During 1840, Thomas turned his thoughts toward spiritual matters in spite of his uncle's worldly influence. He would walk three miles to attend church each Sunday and listen with unabated attention to the longest sermons. He also chose to study the Scriptures carefully to share fully in the joys and duties of the Christian life. As he continually read God's Word, he became quite a student of the Bible. He even taught his good friend Joe Lightburn the truths he learned. Ironically, they both rose to the rank of general on opposite sides during the War Between the States. Lightburn eventually became a Baptist minister after the war. As for the young Tom Jackson, he reportedly considered going into the ministry prior to the war. Thomas, however, was discouraged from following this calling due to his lack of education and his apprehension about speaking in public.

In 1841, Thomas's life changed when he was offered a new position by his Uncle Cummins. On June 11, he was made constable of one half of Lewis County. This seventeen-year-old was now seen with his bag of bills and account books going up and down the hills of the county. In this work, he had to be firm and exact, for it was now his task to collect money due for debts.

The following story is told of his nerve and skill in doing this unpleasant duty. A man

Jackson and the Debtor

who owed a debt of ten dollars promised to pay it at a given time. The day came and the man did not keep his word. Young Jackson paid the money out of his own purse and then watched for the man who would not pay his debt. The very next morning, the man came riding up the street on a good horse. When the man dismounted from his horse, Jackson immediately confronted him with not keeping his word and was going to take the horse for the debt. When the latter resisted, a fierce fight took place in the street. In the midst of the fight, the man mounted his horse and started riding off.

Jackson, however, sprang forward and seized the bridle. Seeing that he could not get the man off the horse in any other way, he led it to the low door of the Weston livery stable. The man hit him right and left with his whip but Jackson clung to the bridle and pulled the horse into the stable. The man was forced to slide off his horse and Jackson was able to seize the animal and the bill was paid.

Though this life in the open air was good for the health of our hero, it did not benefit his morals. He was kept away from home and was thrown with the worst class of people in Lewis County. His Uncle Cummins, moreover, was keeping "bachelor's hall." He kept race horses and nobody except Thomas could ride for him if a contest was close. It was said through all that country that if a horse could win, it would prevail if young Tom Jackson rode him in the race. Young Thomas, therefore, began to spent more time seeking the world's treasures and had less time for the Lord.

This young man was thrown early upon the world without mother or father or any godly influence, except for the preaching and reading of Holy Scripture, to keep him in the right way. In this wild, rough life, God had begun to plant the seed of His Word in the heart of this orphan boy. Even now, the great God, who has said that He will be a father to the fatherless, was opening up a way to make Himself known to young Jackson. Thomas Jackson would come to love the Lord in future years because the Lord first loved him.

Chapter 2

A Cadet

1842–1846

In 1842, the place of a cadet in the United States Military Academy at West Point became vacant. In that school, the young men of the United States are trained to become soldiers. Thomas immediately sought and secured an appointment to this great academy. Very soon he traveled on horseback to Clarksburg where he would take the coach going to Washington. He had so few clothes that his whole wardrobe was packed in a pair of saddlebags.

When he reached Clarksburg, he found that the stagecoach had passed by but he rode on until he overtook it and then continued to the city of Washington. He was met by his friend Mr. Hays, a member of Congress from his district, who took him immediately to the Secretary of War, The latter was so pleased with his manly bearing and direct speech that he ordered his warrant to be made out immediately.

Mr. Hays wished him to stay in Washington for a few days to see the sights of the city; however, he was content to climb to the top of the dome of the Capitol from which he could view the whole scene immediately. He was then ready to continue to West Point for examination. His great concern now was the thought that he might not know enough to pass his entrance examination. Mr. Hays wrote to his friends at the academy and asked them to be easy in examining the mountain boy who ardently wished to be a soldier; therefore, it is said that they asked him very few hard questions. Thomas was now eighteen years old. He had a fresh, ruddy face and was strong and full of courage.

The fourth class men at this school were called by their school-mates "plebs"[1] and were forced to sweep and scrub the barracks and to do other tasks of the same kind. The third-class men would play tricks on the new boys, some of which were quite hard to handle. When they saw this country boy in his homespun clothes, they thought that they could make fun of him. Thomas, however, showed them his courage and good temper which caused his rivals to eventually leave him alone.

Thomas thus turned his efforts toward studying because he had twice as much work to do to catch up with his classmates. He once said to a friend that he studied very hard for what he learned at West Point. Just as when he was a boy, if he did not understand the lesson of the day, he would not pass over it to the next but would work on it until he knew all about it.

1. This term is short for *plebeians* who were members of the ancient Roman lower class; thus *plebs* refers to the common people.

It was often the case that when called to the blackboard to recite, he would say that he was still at work on the last lesson. This caused him to get low marks but he was too honest to pretend to know what he did not understand. His teachers judged his mind sound and strong, but not quick. What he lacked in quickness, he made up in steady work. After the fourth year at West Point, he graduated seventeenth in his class.

During the second year at West Point, he grew, as it were, by a leap to the height of six feet and in his cadet uniform was very fine looking. He was neat in his attire and kept his gun clean and bright. It is said that one day during this year, he found that his bright musket had been stolen and that a dirty and rusty one had been put in its place.

Thomas told the captain of his loss and gave him a mark by which his gun might be known. That evening it was found in the hands of a fellow cadet who had stolen it and then told a falsehood to shield himself from punishment.

Jackson was angry that his musket had been stolen but was even more enraged at the falsehood; therefore, he asked that the cadet be sent away, as he was unfit to stay at the academy. The friends of the boy at last prevailed upon him to waive his right of pressing the charge and the erring cadet was let alone. Not long after, however, the cadet again broke the rules of the school and was sent away in disgrace. From this, we see that Jackson had a hatred of all that was low and wicked. At that time, he wrote several principles as rules for his life in his journal. They touched on morals, manners, dress, the choice of friends, and the aims of life. One of these rules every boy and girl should keep in mind. It was this:

Winners never quit and quitters never win.

We shall see that this was truly the guiding star of his life. Whatever he willed to do, he always did by the sheer force of determination. At this time, it is plain that it was his purpose to place his

Bird's-eye View of Mexico City

name high up on the roll of earthly honor. Beneath his shy and modest manners, there burned the wish to be truly great. His life was not yet ruled by the love of Christ but it showed some high and noble aims. Jackson was twenty-two years old when he left West Point, June 30, 1846. Upon graduating, he took the rank of second lieutenant of the artillery in the United States army. The artillery is that branch of an army which fights with cannons, or big guns. During that time, a war was going on between the United States and Mexico. General Winfield Scott was chosen to take the chief command of the United States army and Jackson, the young lieutenant, was sent to join him in the south of Mexico.

Chapter 3

A Major of Artillery

1847–1850

O n the ninth day of March 1847, thirteen thousand five hundred troops were landed in one day from the American fleet upon the seashore near Veracruz (Ve′rä kroos′), Mexico. This fine army, with its waving flags and bright guns, presented a scene of splendor which Lieutenant Jackson never forgot. General Scott's plan was to take the city of Veracruz by storm and then march over the hills and lofty mountains to the City of Mexico. The fighting in Mexico was very hard and many soldiers lost their lives.

On the thirteenth of March, General Scott had placed his men all around Veracruz and was ready for battle. On the twenty-ninth of March, after a fierce battle, the city was taken by the Americans. This was the first battle in which our hero took part; it is said that Lieutenant Jackson fought bravely.

From Veracruz, the army marched on until it came to a large mountain. On the crest of that mountain stood a strong fort called Cerro Gordo (Ser′-ro Gôr′-do). From there,

Captain Robert E. Lee

Captain Robert E. Lee led American troops over a rough road to the rear of the Mexican line. Since the Americans were in front of and also behind the Mexicans, the latter were soon put to flight—leaving many men and guns on the battlefield. After this battle, Jackson was placed in the light artillery which used small cannons and moved rapidly from place to place.

This job was just what young Jackson wanted because the light artillery service, though more dangerous, gave him a better chance to win the honors for which his soul thirsted. Santa Anna, the general of the Mexicans, now brought forward another large army and placed it on the mountain heights of Cherubusco. Here, a fierce fight took place and the Mexicans were again driven back. As a reward for his brave conduct in this fight, our hero was given the rank of captain of artillery. The army then marched on over the mountains to the strong castle of Chapultepec (Chä-pool´ta-pek´). This castle was built upon a high hill guarding the plain which led to the City of Mexico. The level plain at the foot of the mountain was covered with crops of corn and other grain and with groves of trees. Here and there were deep and wide ditches which the farmers had dug for drains. These ditches the artillery and horsemen could not cross. In fact, the growing crops so hid them that the men could not see them until they had reached their brinks. Within the castle of Chapultepec were swarms of Mexican soldiers while around its base were cannons that guarded every road that led to it.

On the thirteenth of September, the assault was made concurrently on three sides. Jackson was sent with his men and guns to the northwest side of the castle. Two regiments of infantry, or footmen, marched with him. They pushed forward, pouring shot and shell at their foe until they were quite close to the Mexican guns. At such a short range, Jackson instantly found a number of his men struck down or scattered and his horses killed by the storm of grapeshot. Just at that moment, General Worth, saw how closely pressed Jackson was and sent word to fall back. Jackson, however, replied that if

General Worth would send him fifty more men he would march forward and take the guns which had done such deadly work.

Jackson Moving a Cannon Across a Ditch

While the troops were coming up, it is said that Jackson lifted a gun by hand across a deep ditch and began to fire upon the Mexicans with the help of only one man— the rest of his command being either killed, wounded, or hidden in the ditch.

Soon another cannon was moved across the ditch and, in a few moments, the foe was driven back by the rapid firing of these two guns. By this time, the men storming the castle on the other two sides had fought their way in and the Mexicans began to fall back upon the City of Mexico.

Orders had been given that when this move took place, the artillery should move forward rapidly and scatter the ranks of the foe. In an instant Jackson's guns were thundering after the Mexicans fleeing through the gates into the city. The next morning, September 14, the gates were forced and the Americans marched into the city of Mexico.

For his brave conduct in the Battle of Chapultepec, Jackson was promoted to the rank of major.

In later years, when he was modestly telling of this battle, a young man cried out, "Major, why did you not run when so many of your men and horses were killed?" He replied, with a quiet smile, "I was not ordered to do

Capture of the Mexican Battery

so. If I had been ordered to run I would have done so." Once, when asked by a friend if he felt no fear when so many were falling around him, he said that he felt only a great desire to perform some brave deed that would win for him lasting fame. At that time, his thoughts were chiefly fixed upon the faithful performance of his duty and gaining honor and distinction by his labor.

Storming of Chapultepec

In the beautiful Mexico City, the American army now rested from warfare. Some months passed before Jackson's command was ordered home. His duties being light, he began the study of the Spanish language and was soon able to speak it well. He greatly enjoyed the fine climate of Mexico and admired the beauty and grace of her women. For the first time in his life, he also began to think often of God and to study the Bible in search of the truth.

On May 26, 1848, a treaty of peace was made between the United States and Mexico, that officially ended the war. A short time later, the American troops were sent home. Major Jackson's command was sent to Fort Hamilton, about seven miles from the city of New York. While there, he was baptized and began to live his life for the glory of Christ. God had changed the heart of this brave soldier and gave him wisdom to see that life should be lived for the glory of God—not for the glory of self.

After he had been at Fort Hamilton two years, Major Jackson was sent to Fort Meade, near Tampa Bay, on the west coast of Florida. On March 28, 1851, while stationed in Florida, he was elected professor of natural and experimental philosophy and artillery tactics at the Military Institute at Lexington, Virginia.

Thomas J. Jackson at Age Twenty-four

A Military Fort of the Time

Chapter 4

A Professor

1851–1860

In writing of Major Jackson as a professor, it seems entirely appropriate to mention the circumstances leading to his appointment to that teaching position.

As you have already read, Jackson was raised in adverse circumstances which prevented him in early youth from receiving the benefits of a consistently good education. Primarily through his own efforts at home, he prepared himself to enter the United States Military Academy at West Point. His first year's course would have discouraged him in completing his studies had he not been conscious of the fact that the Lord would supply all of his needs according to His riches in glory. In his second year, he raised his general standing as a student from 51 to 30; in the third, from 30 to 20; and in the fourth, his graduating year, from 20 to 17. His upward progress attracted attention and one of his associates remarked "Had Jackson remained at West Point another four years longer, he would have reached the head of his class."

His advancement in the Mexican war, rising rapidly from second lieutenant of artillery to major, was noticed by many at the academy. His gallant services had been heralded to the world through the official reports of his superiors.

General Francis H. Smith, superintendent of the Virginia Military Institute, in the "Institute Memorial," writes:

> It is not surprising that, when the Board of Visitors of the Virginia Military Institute were looking for a suitable person to fill the chair of Natural and Experimental Philosophy and Artillery, the associates of this young and brave major of artillery should have pointed him out as worthy to receive so distinguished an honor. Other

names had been submitted to the Board of visitors by the Faculty of West Point, all men distinguished for high scholarship and for gallant services in Mexico. McClellan, Reno, Rosecrans, afterward generals in the Northern army, and G. W. Smith, who afterward became a general in the Confederate army, were named. But the peculiar fitness of young Jackson, the high testimonials to his personal character, and his nativity as a Virginian, satisfied the Board that they might safely choose him for the vacant chair without seeking candidates from other states. He was, therefore, unanimously elected to the professorship on the twenty-eighth of March 1851 and entered upon the duties of his chair on the first of September.

The professional career of Major Jackson was marked by great faithfulness and by an unobtrusive, yet earnest spirit. With high mental endowments, teaching was a new profession to him and demanded, in the important department of instruction assigned to him, an amount of labor which, from the state of his health, and especially from the weakness of his eyes, he rendered at great sacrifice.

Conscientious fidelity to duty marked every step of his life here and, when called to active duty in the field, he had made considerable progress in the preparation of an elementary work on optics which he proposed to publish for the benefit of his classes.

Strict and sometimes stern in his discipline, though ever polite and kind, he was not always a popular professor, but no professor ever had to a higher degree the confidence and respect of the cadets for his unbending integrity and fearlessness in the discharge of his duty. If he was exact in his demands upon them, they knew he was no less so in his own respect for and submission to authority, and it became a proverb among them that it was useless to write an excuse for a report made by Major Jackson. His great principle of government was that a *general* rule should not be violated for any particular good and his *steady* rule as a teacher was that a man could always complete what he was willing to do.

Punctual to a minute, I have known him to walk in front of the superintendent's quarters in a hard rain, because the hour had not quite come when it was his duty to present his weekly class reports.

Virginia Military Institute Barracks

For ten years, he conducted his unwearied labors as a professor, making during this period such a good impression upon those who occasionally were under his command that, when the War Between the States broke out, the spontaneous desire of all cadets and graduates was, to serve under him as their leader.

An incident is related by General Smith in the same work which shows clearly how Jackson was looked upon in the community in which he resided:

> He left the Virginia Military Institute on the twenty-first of April 1861 in command of the corps of cadets and reported for duty at Camp Lee, Richmond. Dangers were thickening rapidly around the state. Invasion by overwhelming numbers seemed imminent. Norfolk, Richmond, Alexandria, and Harpers Ferry were threatened. Officers were needed to command at these points. The Governor of Virginia nominated Major Jackson as the colonel of volunteers. His nomination was immediately and unanimously confirmed by the Council of State and sent to the Convention then in session. Some prejudice existed in that body from the supposed influence of the Virginia Military Institute in these appointments and the question was asked by various members, 'Who is this Thomas J. Jackson?' A member of the Convention from the county of Rockbridge, Hon. S. McDowell Moore, replied: 'I can tell you who he is. If you put Jackson in command at Norfolk, he will never leave it unless you order him to do so.' Such was the impression made upon his neighbors and friends in his quiet life as a professor at the Military Institute. In accepting the position of professor, he was again stepping higher. In active warfare, an officer may advance rapidly but, in times of peace, he lives quietly at a military post and simply rusts out. Ill health, brought on mainly by exposure in the Mexican War, caused Major Jackson to resign his commission in the army but, in all probability, had this not been the case, he would have abandoned army life because he felt that, by close study and application, he could reach a much higher

degree of mental excellence than he had gained, and the position of professor would enable him to do this for he knew that the best way to learn was to teach.

In consequence of the weakness of his eyes, his great willpower had now to be exerted to the utmost because he could not use his eyes at night. To do himself and his classes justice, each morning after class hours, he would carefully read over the lessons for the next day and, at night after his simple supper, he would quietly sit with his face to the wall and study in his mind the lessons read that day. In this way he made them his own and was ready to teach the next day. This training was of great use to him in his life as a soldier. The power of his mind was such that while riding, in later years, at the head of his army, he could study the movements of the foe and plan his own with as much care and skill as in the quiet of his study at home.

The statement made by General Smith, respecting the wish of the cadets to serve under Major Jackson in the war, shows how popular he was. This estimate of his powers could have been produced only by their knowledge of his great worth.

"Old Jack" was the name given to the Major by the cadets, however, it was never used derisively. Pranks were played in Major Jackson's section room by the cadets but more for their own amusement than for any other purpose. They well knew the consequences if caught but were willing to run the risk for the sake of fun.

Cadet Abe Fulkerson once wore a collar made out of three fourths of a yard of linen for no other purpose than to pro-

Cadet at the Institute

duce a laugh and it made even "Old Jack" laugh—that is, smile, which he would not have done if the size, shape, or color of collars had been fixed by the Institute regulations.

Cadet Davidson Penn, with an uncommonly solemn face and apparently in good faith, once asked Major Jackson, "Major, can a cannon be so bent to make it shoot around a corner?" The Major showed not the slightest sign of impatience or of merriment but, after a moment of apparently sober thought, replied, "Mr. Penn, I reckon hardly."

It has been said, moreover, that Major Jackson never smiled or laughed. It has just been shown, however, that he did smile once. Undoubtedly, when he read the excuse mentioned below, not only would another smile have been seen but a good, hearty laugh heard as well. At artillery drill one evening, Major Jackson had given the command, "Limbers and caissons[2] pass your pieces, trot, march!" Cadet Hambrick did not trot at command and was reported. The next day, the following excuse was submitted:

> Report: Cadet Hambrick not trotting at artillery drill.
>
> Excuse: I am a natural pacer.

These three incidents are recounted by Dr. J. C. Hiden, of Richmond, Virginia.

Cadet Thomas B. Amiss, who was afterwards a surgeon in one of Jackson's Georgian regiments, tried a trick for the double purpose of evading a recitation and creating a laugh. He was squad marcher of his section and, after calling the roll and making his report to the officer of the day, he turned the section over to the next man on the roll, took his place in ranks, and cautioned the new squad marcher not to report him absent. While the squad marcher was making his

---

2. Here, *limbers* and *caissons* refer to infantry in charge of ammunition and the equipment used to transport it. A *limber* is a two-wheeled, detachable front part of a gun carriage, usually supporting an ammunition chest, or *caisson*; it originally was pulled by four or six horses, behind which was towed a field gun or a two-wheeled ammunition wagon, also called a *caisson*.

report to Major Jackson, whose eyes seemed always riveted to his class book when this was being done, Amiss noiselessly climbed to the top of a column that stood nearly in the center of the room. Having received the report, Major Jackson began to call the names of those whom he wished to recite at the board, beginning with Amiss. Not hearing Amiss respond, he asked, "Mr. Amiss absent?" The squad marcher replied, "No, sir." The Major looked steadily along the line of faces, seemed perplexed, and cast his eyes upwards, when he spied the delinquent at the top of the column. For a moment, the Major gazed at the clinging figure and said, "You stay there." Amiss had to stay where he was until the recitation was over. He was reported, court-martialed, received the maximum number of demerits, and had many extra tours of guard duty assigned him. During the walking of these tours, in the lone hours of the night, he had ample time to repent of his folly.

When the class that graduated in 1860 began its recitations under Major Jackson, a sudden end was made to all kinds of merriment in his classroom. A member of the class, however, who was later a member of Congress from Virginia, hid a small music box under his coat and carried it into the classroom. After the recitation had started, he touched a spring and the room was filled with sweet, muffled strains of music. Major Jackson did not hear, or if he did, took no notice of it. The cadet, finding that his music was not duly appreciated, began to bark in very low tones like a puppy and, when this met with the same fate as the music, he became more bold and barked louder. Major Jackson, without raising his voice above an ordinary tone, said, "Mr. C., when you march the section in again, please leave that puppy outside." The laugh was on the young cadet.

The following incident illustrates clearly how little Major Jackson regarded public opinion or personal feeling when it came in conflict with duty. A young cadet was dismissed through a circumstance that happened in Major Jackson's classroom. The young man became so enraged that he challenged the Major to fight a duel and sent him word that if the Major would not fight he would kill him on sight. Actuated solely by conscientious motives, Major Jackson took the necessary precautions to prevent a conflict and informed the young man through his friends that if he was attacked by the cadet he would defend himself. Although the Major passed back and forth as usual, the attack was not made. This same cadet was under Jackson's command during the War Between the States and, before the close of the war, commanded the "Stonewall Brigade" which was made eminently famous by Jackson. In later years, when asked his opinion of this great man, he said that Jackson was the only man ever born who had never been whipped.

Major Jackson seemed to enjoy the duty of drilling the artillery battery more than any other duty he had to do. It was natural that he should, for he had won fame as an artillery officer in the Mexican War.

Near the close of every session of the Institute, Major Jackson was required to drill the battery before the Board of Visitors. To make it more interesting to the public, always present in large crowds, blank cartridges were fired and the drill was given the semblance of a battery in actual battle. An impressive scene was witnessed at this drill in 1860. It started at 5:00 P.M. Major Jackson had put the battery through its various movements and, as the time approached for the firing to begin, he seemed more and more interested in his work. His old professor of engineering at West Point, Dennis Mahan, and the commandant of cadets of that institution, Colonel Hardee, witnessed the drill. Shortly after the commencement of the cannon drill, dark clouds began to gather in the west and the rumbling of thunder could be heard. The firing began and all was excitement. Closer and closer came the clouds and the artillery of heaven seemed to reply to the discharges of the battery. Major Jackson had been slowly retreating before the imaginary foe, firing by half battery. A cloud came nearer and nearer, unheeded by

Jackson. Suddenly, his voice rang clear and sharp, "Fire advancing by half battery"—the foe was retreating—"right-half battery advance, commence firing!" New positions were rapidly taken and the firing was at its height. Then the storm broke in all its fury. Up to that time the Major had seemed oblivious to all, save the drill. The bursting storm brought him to himself and he dismissed the battery which immediately went to shelter. Major Jackson stood where he was, folded his arms, and stood like a statue in the driving storm. An umbrella was sent to him from a house close by with an invitation to come to cover. He replied, "No, thank you;" and there he stood until the storm was over, doubtless thinking of the hard fought fields of Mexico and the bloodshed he had seen in combat.

It was during these days as a soldier in Mexico that Jackson began to search carefully for the truth that can only be found in Christ Jesus. In the fall of 1851, Major Jackson came in contact with John Blair Lyle who was the owner of a Lexington bookshop which Jackson ofttimes visited. Mr. Lyle recognized in him a desire to know more about Christ and His gospel, so he put him in touch with Dr. William S. White of the Lexington Presbyterian Church. Reverend White opened the Scriptures to the Major, explaining God's free offer of salvation through faith in Christ Jesus. On November 22, 1851, Major Jackson made a public profession of faith and became a member of the Lexington Presbyterian Church. Jackson's faith and service to Christ—and to the wider cause of Christianity—was the most dynamic aspect of his character from that time until his death twelve years later.

His chief desire was now to bring his entire life under the lordship of Jesus Christ. In February 1852, he was made a deacon and given a class of young men in the Sunday school. Many of his young students came to know Jesus Christ as their personal Savior. Jackson, moreover, grew in his love for the truths he found in the Bible. He also gathered together the African slaves of the town every Sabbath evening to teach them the truths contained in God's

Word. He soon had a school of about one hundred pupils and twelve teachers. He maintained contact with his pupils from 1855 to 1861, when he left Lexington to enter the Confederate army. Until his death, it was always a great pleasure for him to hear about the spiritual progress that his Sabbath school students were making—whether they were black or white.

Now more than ever, duty became the rule of his life—duty to God and duty to man. So great was his regard for the Sabbath that he would not even read a letter or mail one which he knew would be carried on that day. The Rev. R. L. Dabney tells us that one Sabbath, when a dear friend, who knew that the Major had received a letter from his lady love late on Saturday night, asked, "Major, surely you have read your letter?" "Certainly not," said he. "What obstinacy!" exclaimed his friend. "Do you not think that your desire to know its contents will distract your mind from divine worship far more than if you had simply read it?" "No," answered Jackson, quietly, "I shall make the most faithful effort I can to control my thoughts and, as I do this from a sense of duty, I shall expect the divine blessing upon it."

When a single man, he made it a rule to accept, if possible, all invitations, saying that when a friend had taken the trouble to invite him, it was his duty to attend. Major Gittings, once a cadet and a relative of Major Jackson, says:

> Speaking from a social standpoint, no man ever had a more delicate regard for the feelings of others than he and nothing would embarrass him more than any evil that might happen to cause pain or distress of mind to others. Hence, he was truly a polite man and yet, while his manner was often constrained and even awkward, he would usually make a favorable impression through his wish to please.

When Major Jackson first came to Lexington, he was in ill health and many things he did were looked upon as odd which were really not so. He had been at a famous hospital in the North. He was told to go to bed at nine o'clock. If that hour found him at a party or lecture, or any other place, in order to obey his physician, he would leave.

The indigestion problems with which he suffered often caused drowsiness and he would sometimes go to sleep while talking to a friend. Before leaving Lexington, he seemed to have gained complete control over his muscles even while he was asleep, for no one, in the few years preceding his departure, ever saw his head and his knees in contact. It was a common thing, however, to see him sound asleep while sitting perfectly upright.

Before marriage, Major Jackson had his room in the barracks but took his meals at a hotel in Lexington. It has been said by some that his odd habits made much comment and that he was laughed at and insulted by rude, cruel persons. This could hardly have been true, for an insult offered to "Old Jack" would certainly have been found out in some way and, if not resented personally, it would have been resented by the cadets to a man. During the four years that Major Jackson made his home in Lexington, many individuals who lived there clearly have stated that they had never heard of these insults. Surely, had they ever been given, they would have been talked about, because Jackson's name was on every tongue and the incidents of his life, from boyhood to death, were a common subject of conversation.

Though Major Jackson was very modest, few men ever relied more fully upon their God-given abilities. Jackson believed that he could do all things through Jesus Christ who strengthened him. Mentioning one day to a friend that he was going to begin the study of Latin, he received the reply that one who had not studied the forms of that language in youth could never become master of it in later years. To this Jackson replied, "No, if I try it, I believe that God will enable me to master the language."

This stern willpower came to the aid of his ambition often. He found it difficult to speak in public. To acquire the art, he joined a literary club called the "Franklin Society." He was always at the meetings and spoke in his turn. At first, however, his efforts were painful both to himself and to his hearers. His health was poor, his nerves were unstrung, and sometimes he was so confused that he would break down in the middle of a sentence trying to think of the right word. When this happened, he would quietly sit down and, when his turn in the debate came again, would rise and make another try. Before the close of the debate, therefore, he would succeed in telling what was in his mind. By trying continually, he became a good speaker.

Soon after joining the Presbyterian church, good Dr. White, his pastor, called upon him to pray in public. He prayed in such a halting way that Dr. White told him that he would never again ask him to perform such a hard task. Major Jackson replied that it was a cross to him to pray in public but that he had made up his mind to bear it and did not wish to be excused. He persisted and soon became a leader in prayer. Indeed, during the remainder of his life he was a devout prayer warrior.

General Hill, speaking of this incident, says:

> I think his conduct here was due to his determination to conquer every weakness of his nature. He once told me that when he was a small boy, being sick, a mustard plaster was placed upon his chest and his guardian mounted him upon a horse to go to a neighbor's house, so that his mind might be diverted and the plaster kept on. He said that the pain was so dreadful that he fainted soon after getting off his horse. I asked him if he had kept it on to obey his guardian. He answered, 'No, it was owing to a feeling that I have had from childhood not to yield to trials and difficulties.'

The same close friend also writes:

> Dr. Dabney thinks that he was timid and that nothing but his iron

will made him brave. I think this is a mistake. The muscles of his
face would twitch when a battle was about to open and his hand
would tremble so that he could hardly write. His men would see
the working of his face and would say, 'Old Jack is making faces at
the Yankees.' But all this only showed weak nerves. I think he loved
danger for its own sake.

Like the Apostle Paul, he kept his body under guard and would
not let any appetite control him or any weakness overcome him.
He used neither coffee, tobacco, nor spirits, and he would go all
winter without cloak or overcoat in the mountains of Virginia, giving as a reason that he did not wish to give in to the cold. For this
same reason, he never drank spirits of any kind. It is told of him
that once during the War Between the States, when he was too near
the outposts of the foe to have a fire and being greatly chilled, he
was advised by his surgeon to take a drink of brandy. At length, he
agreed to take some but made such a sour face in swallowing it that
some one asked him if it choked him. "No," he replied, "I like it.
That is the reason I never use it." Another time, being asked to take
a drink of brandy, he said, "No; I thank you; I am more afraid of it
than all the Federal bullets." The courageous Jackson afraid of
strong drink! What a lesson to people who have not the courage to
say "No," when tempted to do wrong!

In the midst of this busy life as professor, Major Jackson was
married, on August 4, 1853, to Miss Eleanor Junkin, the daughter
of the president of Washington College, Lexington, Virginia. This
lovely lady lived only fourteen months after her marriage. Major
Jackson's grief at her death was so great that it alarmed his friends.
His health, never good, suffered so seriously that his friends
induced him in the summer of 1856 to take a trip to Europe, hoping that the grief might be broken which bound him to sadness.

His European trip benefited him considerably in health and spirits. With great zeal, he decided to resume his labors in his classes at

both the Military Institute and the Sunday school. As he started on his return trip, however, storms prevented him from reaching the institute on its opening date of September 1, which he had promised to do. Although he had set out in plenty of time, he arrived late. A lady friend, knowing what a slave he was to his word, asked him if he had not been miserable at the delay. The answer was characteristic of the man. He had done his part; Providence had intervened and he had not worried in the least. Few men ever trusted Providence more implicitly than Jackson and, when he went to God in prayer, he knew that his feet would be guided in the right way.

Dr. Dabney tells us that one day, when a friend said that he could not understand how one could "pray without ceasing," Jackson replied that, for some time, he had been in the habit of praying all through the day. "When we take our meals," said he, "there is grace; and when I take a draft of water, I always pause to lift up my heart to God in thanks for the water of life; and when I go to my classroom and await the coming of the cadets that is my time to pray for them—and so with every other act of the day." We see that Jackson was truly a "praying man." His pastor, Rev. Dr. White, once said that Major Jackson was the happiest man that he had ever known. This happiness came from his faith in the saving care of God. We are told that a friend once said to him, "Suppose you should lose your eyesight and then, too, be very ill and have to depend on those bound to you by no tie. Would this be too much for your faith? Do you think you could be happy then?" He thought a moment and then said, "If it was the will of God to place me on a sick bed, He would enable me to lie there in peace a hundred years."

Such was the faith of this great man. As he grew older his spirit became more saintly until, when called upon to go up higher to meet his Lord, his end seemed more like a passing over than a death.

Major Jackson's Home in Lexington

Major Jackson was married again, on July 15, 1857, to Mary Anna Morrison, the daughter of Dr. R. H. Morrison, a Presbyterian minister, from North Carolina. Shortly after his second marriage, Major Jackson bought a house and a few acres of land and soon all his spare time was spent in working in his garden and fields. We are told that his little farm of rocky hill land was soon well fenced and tilled by the labor of hands. He liked to have his friends visit him and nowhere else was he as easy and happy as with guests at his own table.

In his home, military sternness left his brow and the law of love took its place. This story is told of him which shows how gentle and tender a soldier may be. "Once a friend, who was taking his little four-year-old girl on a journey without her mother, called on the way to spend the night with Major Jackson. At bed time, when Mrs. Jackson wished to take the child to her room for the night, the father replied that his little one would give less trouble if he kept her with him. In the still watches of the night, he heard a soft step and felt a hand laid upon his bed. It was Major Jackson, who, fearing that the little girl would toss off the covering, came to see that all was safe."

This good and peaceful life at Lexington was short. The black cloud of civil war was hovering over the land and the storm finally burst in great fury, sweeping Major Jackson away from his quiet life, his professorial duties, and his beloved wife and friends into the midst of carnage and death and to deeds that made him famous worldwide.

Major Jackson had but one more duty to perform as a professor and officer of the Virginia Military Institute. He had been left in charge of the corps of cadets when the superintendent had been called to Richmond. Early on the morning of Sunday, April 21, 1861, an order was received by Major Jackson from Governor John Letcher, directing him to leave with his command for Richmond at 12:30 P.M. that day. Major Jackson's arrangements were promptly made and he sent a request to his pastor, good Dr. White, to come to the Institute and hold religious services for the young men before their departure. These services were held in front of the barracks. The battalion was drawn up in line of battle, Major Jackson at the head and venerable Dr. White in the front and center. All, with bowed heads, were devoutly listening to the invocations speeding heavenward. The clock in the Institute tower gave the signal for departure and, a few moments later, Jackson took up the line of march and left his beloved pastor.

The keynote of his great success as a soldier was prompt obedience to orders and requiring the same of others.

Chapter 5

A Confederate Colonel

Spring 1861

B efore continuing with the life of our hero, I must tell you, in a few plain and truthful words, the causes of the war which, in 1861, broke out between the states.

Perhaps you will remember that, after the Revolutionary War, the thirteen colonies voluntarily agreed to form a Union and adopted a set of laws called the Constitution of the United States.

From the very beginning, however, the States found it hard to agree. Laws which suited one section did not suit another, therefore, some just cause for a quarrel was often warranted. The men who wrote the Constitution, for example, could not agree on the best way to handle the issue of slavery. As a result, the compromise that they reached merely provided a temporary solution to a major dilemma that affected each of the states.

Eventually, the question of slavery seemed to give the most trouble. As you probably have been told, African slaves were first brought to Virginia in 1619 by the Dutch and then afterwards by the English and other European traders, until all the colonies held slaves. The cold climate of the North, however, did not suit the African slaves who were used to a warmer climate. Over a period of time, they were sold by northern businessmen to Southern planters who put them to work in cotton and tobacco fields.

In the sunny South, the slaves were often treated better than in the North and, in 1861, numbered about four million. Having sold their slaves to Southern planters, some people in the North and West began to think that it was a sin to hold the Negroes in bondage. These people began to make laws affecting the people in the South. Many leaders in the South believed that the Northern lawmakers were hypocrites who cared little if the farmers in the South went bankrupt. Although the Southern leaders were often justified in their political and economic concerns, they were too proud to admit that slavery on the basis of race is morally wrong.

The Southern leaders foolishly and stubbornly insisted that Negro slaves were nothing more than the "property of the plantation owner." Perhaps these leaders forgot that America was established to be one nation, under God, with liberty and justice for *all*.

This event cast great gloom over the country. Many persons in the North thought that they were a martyr to the cause of slavery while the people in the South felt that they could no longer enjoy in peace and safety the rights granted to them by the U.S. Constitution. The Southern people were, for the most part, willing to abolish slavery in their part of the country as long as they could do it on their own terms—not on terms dictated to them by the central government.

Major Jackson was truly Southern in feeling. He believed in "States' rights" and that the South should take her stand and resist all efforts to coerce and crush her. He, however, dreaded war and thought it the duty of Christians throughout the land to pray for peace. In addition, he had his own conviction that slavery for racial reasons was morally wrong. Like most people in the South, Jackson did not own slaves.

A month before South Carolina went out of the Union, Major Jackson called upon his pastor, Dr. White, and said: "It is painful to know how carelessly they speak of war. If the government insists upon the measures now threatened, there must be war. They seem not to know what its horrors are. Let us have meetings to pray for peace." Dr. White agreed to his request and the burden of Major Jackson's prayer was that God would preserve the land from civil war.

In November 1860, after Mr. Abraham Lincoln was elected President, the Southern States saw no hope of having their voice heard or their objectives met, thus they resolved to secede, or withdraw, from the Union. Many Southern leaders sincerely believed that, since each of the states freely and voluntarily joined themselves to the Union, they were equally free to leave.

President Jefferson Davis

South Carolina took the lead and seceded on December 20, 1860. She was quickly followed by Mississippi, Alabama, Florida, Georgia, Louisiana, and Texas. On the ninth of January 1861, these states united and, at Montgomery, Alabama, formed a government called "The Confederate States of America," with Jefferson Davis as President. Virginia was slow to withdraw from the Union formed by the states but, when President Lincoln called for seventy-five thousand soldiers to invade the Southern States, she delayed no longer. On April 17, 1861, she seceded and began to prepare for war. "In one week," says Dabney, "the whole State was changed into a camp." The sons of Virginia rushed to arms and soon Richmond was filled with men drilling and preparing to fight. At daybreak on Sunday morning, April 21, 1861, an order came to Lexington from Governor Letcher of Virginia to march the cadets that day to Richmond. As the senior officers were already in Richmond, Major Jackson immediately prepared to go forward with his corps.

At eleven o'clock in the morning, he went to his home to say goodbye to his wife. They retired to their own room where he read the fifth chapter of Second Corinthians, which begins with these beautiful words: "For we know, if our earthly house of this tabernacle be dissolved, we have a building of God, an house not made with hands, eternal in the heavens."

They then knelt and prayed for themselves and for their dear country, imploring God that it might be His holy will to avert war and bloodshed. He then said goodbye to his wife and left his dear home, never more to return to it. After a few days, his wife went to live at the home of a friend.

Major Jackson and the cadets marched forward to Staunton and then they went by train to Richmond. Immediately they went into camp. From Richmond, Major Jackson wrote to his wife "Colonel

Harpers Ferry

Lee, of the army is here and has been made Major General of the Virginia troops. I regard him a better officer than General Scott."

After a few days, on April 21, Major Jackson was made colonel of the Virginia forces and ordered to take command at Harpers Ferry, a town on the Potomac River where the United States government had a great number of workshops and firearms.

This important place had already been captured by Virginia troops and it was necessary to hold it until the arms and machinery could be moved away.

Just here it may be well to give you a word picture of our hero as he began a career which was to fill the world with his fame.

Colonel Thomas J. Jackson

Jackson was tall and very erect, with large hands and feet. His brow was fair and broad; his eyes were blue placid and clear when their owner was calm but, when he was aroused, dark and flashing. His nose was Roman, his cheeks ruddy, his mouth firm, and his chin covered with a brown beard. Long and rapid was his step and, if he was not a graceful rider, he was a fearless one. In battle, or as he rode along his columns, hat in hand, no figure could be nobler than his—bowing right and left to his soldiers whose shouts arose on high. Few, even of his intimate friends, were conscious of his military genius, therefore, he burst upon the world as a meteor darts across a starlit sky.

On his way to Harpers Ferry, he wrote to his dear wife:

Winchester, April 29, 1861

I expect to leave here about 2:00 P.M. today for Harpers Ferry. I am thankful to say that an ever kind Providence, who causes all things to work together for good to them that love Him, has given me the post which I prefer above all others. To His name be all the praise.

You must not expect to hear from me very often, as I shall have more work than I have ever had in the same time before, but don't be troubled about me, as an ever kind Heavenly Father will give me all needful aid.

Thomas Jackson

"This letter," says a friend, "gives a true idea of his character. He feels within himself the genius and power which make him long to have a separate command but he also feels the need of resting upon his Heavenly Father for aid and support."

Colonel Jackson had been ordered by Major General Lee to organize and drill the men who had gathered at Harpers Ferry and to hold the place as long as possible against the foe.

He went to work with great zeal and, aided by Colonel Maury and Major Preston, soon had the men organized into companies and regiments. As Colonel Jackson was known to have been a brave soldier in the Mexican War, he was readily obeyed by the soldiers in his little army which soon numbered forty-five hundred men.

On the second of May, however, Virginia formally joined the Southern Confederacy and handed over the control of all her soldiers to that government, which bound itself in return to defend Virginia and to pay her troops.

General Joseph E. Johnston was sent on the twenty-third of May by the Confederate Government to take command at Harpers Ferry and Colonel Jackson immediately submitted to General Johnston.

The Virginia regiments at that place—the Second, the Fourth, the Fifth, the Twenty-seventh, and a little later, the Thirty-third, with Pendleten's battery of light field guns—were now organized into a brigade, of which Jackson was made the commander. This was the brigade which, afterwards became famous as the "Stonewall Brigade," did much hard fighting and was to the Southern army what the "Tenth Legion" was to the great Caesar.

General J. E. Johnston

General Johnston soon found out that he could not hold Harpers Ferry against the foe which was now coming up under General Patterson. He therefore burnt the great railroad bridge over the Potomac River at Harpers Ferry and moved away all his guns and stores. Then on Sunday, June 16, he withdrew his little army to Bunker Hill, a place about twelve miles from Winchester. There he offered battle to General Patterson but the latter refused to fight and withdrew to the north bank of the Potomac. This he did, though he writes of it in the following words! "It was a sad work; but I had my orders and my duty was to obey."

Until the second of July, Colonel Jackson with his brigade remained a little north of Martinsburg, having in his front Colonel J. E. B. Stuart with a regiment of cavalry. On that day, General Patterson advanced to meet Jackson who went forward with only one regiment, the Fifth Virginia, a few companies of cavalry, and one light field piece. A sharp skirmish ensued. At last, the foe coming up in large numbers, Jackson fell back to the main body of his troops after having taken forty-five prisoners and killed and wounded many of the enemy. Jackson's loss was only two men killed and ten wounded.

In this battle which is known as that of Haines Farm, Colonel Jackson was, no doubt, the only man in the infantry who had ever been under fire, nevertheless, they all behaved with the greatest coolness and bravery.

Jackson, in this first battle, showed such boldness and such care for the lives of his men that he at once gained a hold upon their esteem.

General Patterson now held Martinsburg; while General Johnston, having come up with the whole army, offered him battle each day. Patterson, however, had other plans and soon moved away.

General Robert E. Lee

While General Johnston was at Winchester watching Patterson's movements, Colonel Jackson received this note:

Richmond, July 3rd, '61

My Dear General:

I have the pleasure of sending you a commission of Brigadier General in the provisional Army and to feel that you merit it. May your advancement increase your usefulness to the State.

Very Truly,

R. E. Lee.

General Jackson, for thus we must call him, was very pleased at this promotion and wrote to his wife:

Through the blessing of God, I have now all that I should wish in the line of promotion. May His blessing rest on you is my fervent prayer.

The supreme fact in the character of Jackson was that God came first in all his thoughts. All of his daily decisions, whether it was on or off the battlefield, were made with reference to the truth of Scripture and the Christian faith. All who came to know General Jackson also came to know his abiding faith in the living God of the Holy Bible. He refused to make God irrelevant in any aspect of his being, therefore, he lived a safe and happy life despite his routine hardships.

How inevitably came his humility. Jackson owed all to God—all that he was and all that he had attained in the classroom or battle-field—unto Him alone belonged all the praise and glory. General Jackson wrote from the field: "God has given us a brilliant victory at Harpers Ferry today, may we be thankful for His rich blessings."

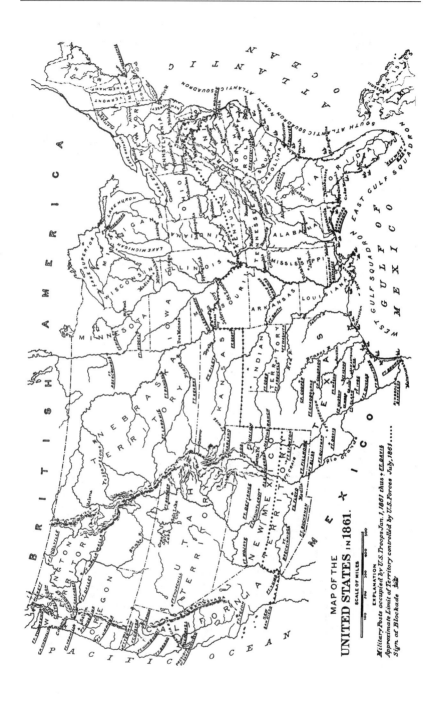

MAP OF THE
UNITED STATES IN 1861.

SCALE OF MILES

EXPLANATION

Military Posts occupied by U.S.Troops Jan. 1, 1861 thus ⋆ ELDAVIS
Approximate Limit of Territory controlled by U.S.Forces July,1861 ......
Sign. of Blockade

Chapter 6

A Brigadier General

1861

During the spring of 1861, the States of North Carolina, Tennessee, and Arkansas, also left the Union and joined the new Confederacy, the capital of which was now Richmond, Virginia.

The great object of the North was to capture Richmond. The Northern leaders therefore raised four large armies to invade Virginia. The first was to go through Fortress Monroe, the second was to advance through Manassas, the third was to march up the Shenandoah Valley, and the forth was to come from the northwest.

Turn to the map of Virginia and find the places which have been mentioned above and you will understand the plan at once.

Now the Confederate army was much smaller than the Federal army because the Southern States were thinly settled, while the North contained very many large cities and had the world from

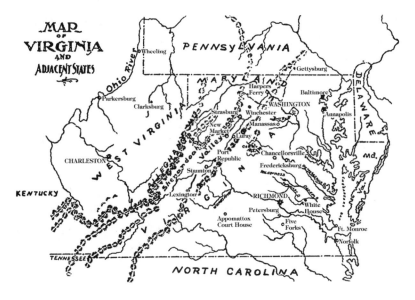

MAP of VIRGINIA AND ADJACENT STATES

which to draw supplies of men and weapons of war. The North also was rich because it had the treasury of the United States, while the South was poor in both money and arms and had the outside world closed off to her. The Confederate leaders, therefore, had to use great skill in meeting such large armies with so few men.

You remember from the last chapter that General Johnston, with a small force, was at Winchester watching General Patterson. Just across the mountains, sixty miles southeast at Manassas, Beauregard (bo-re-gard), another famous Southern general,

Confederate Money

was facing a large Northern army under General McDowell. This army was thirty-five thousand strong while the Confederates had only twenty-eight thousand men. General McDowell's army was composed of the best soldiers in the Northern States and they had splendid firearms, artillery, uniforms, and, in fact, all that money could buy to help them win the battle.

The Confederates, however, were poorly clothed and had old muskets and cannons; many of the cavalry had only the shotguns which they had used for hunting in their boyhood days.

The North fully expected that this fine army would crush the Confederates with one blow, and, when General McDowell was marching forward to battle, he began to cry, "On to Richmond."

Large crowds of reporters, members of Congress, government officials, and even ladies went from Washington to the rear of the Federal army to witness the defeat of the Confederates.

General Beauregard now sent word to General Johnston to leave Patterson and come across the mountains to his aid. General Johnston immediately sent Colonel Stuart, with his cavalry, to face Patterson and to try to keep him from finding out that Johnston had left Winchester and had gone to the help of Beauregard.

General P. G. T. Beauregard

This order Stuart obeyed so well that Johnston reached Manassas, sixty miles away, before Patterson discovered the ploy. General Johnston's army set out from Winchester on the morning of Thursday, July 18. The First Virginia Brigade, led by General Jackson, headed the procession.

MARCHES TO FIRST BULL RUN
Strength of Forces
Patterson: 15,000   Mc Dowell: 35,000
Johnston: 11,000   Beauregard: 22,000

When they had marched about three miles, General Johnston called a halt and an order was read to them explaining that they were going to help Beauregard, who was just starting a great battle with McDowell. The General hoped that his troops would act like men and save their country.

At these words, the men filled the air with their shouts and went forward at double-quick.[3] They waded the Shenandoah River which was waist deep, crossed the Blue Ridge Mountains at Ashby's Gap, and, some hours after night, paused to rest for awhile at the vil-

Wading the Shenandoah River

lage of Paris on the eastern slope of the mountains.

"Let the poor fellows sleep; I will guard the camp myself."

Dr. Dabney, who was part of Jackson's brigade, tells us that, while the men slept, Jackson himself kept watch, saying, "Let the poor fellows sleep; I will guard the camp myself." For two hours he paced up and down under the trees or sat on the fence. At last, an hour before daybreak, he gave up his watch to a member of his staff and, rolling himself upon the grass, was soon fast asleep.

At break of day, the brigade was up and away and, by dusk on July 19, the whole command, dusty, hungry, and

3. A very quick marching pace; the same as *double time* which is a marching cadence of 180 three-foot steps a minute; the normal cadence is 120 steps per minute.

footsore, marched into an old pine field near Manassas where they
spent Saturday resting for the coming battle.

The Confederate lines stretched for eight miles along the southern bank of Bull Run which could be crossed at several places. At
these forts, General Beauregard had placed large bodies of men. On
July 18, before Jackson had come up, General McDowell had tried
to take these forts but his troops had been driven back.

McDowell then made a plan to march a part of his forces around
the Confederates' left wing at a certain stone bridge and to attack
their rear position. Being between two large forces, the Confederates would be crushed or forced to surrender.

On Sunday morning,
July 21, General
McDowell sent forward a
portion of his troops to
the stone bridge which
was guarded then by the
gallant Colonel Evans
with only eleven hun-
dred men. After he had
fought desperately for
several hours and just as
he was outflanked and

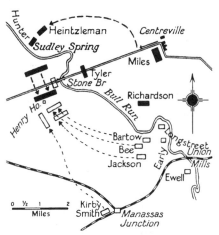

badly bruised, Generals Bee and Bartow came to his aid and for
awhile turned the tide of battle.

Eventually, however, the Confederates were slowly forced back
by larger numbers. At this moment, General Jackson reached the
spot with his brigade of two thousand six hundred men. These he
quickly placed on the crest of a ridge at the edge of a pine thicket
and before them posted seventeen cannons.

Generals Bee and Bartow and Colonel Evans rallied their back
lines on the right, while on the left were a few regiments of Virginia
and Carolina troops. The whole force numbered about six thou-

sand five hundred men. The infantry of this brigade were ordered by Jackson to lie down behind the artillery to escape the fire of the enemy who were now coming across the valley and up the hill with twenty thousand men and twenty-four cannons. Just then, Generals Johnston and Beauregard galloped to the front and cheered the men on in every part of the field.

From 11:00 A.M. until 3:00 P.M., the artillery shook the earth with its dreadful roar and thousands of musket balls whizzed through the air, black with the smoke of battle.

While the artillery fight was continuing, General Jackson rode back and forth between the guns and his regiments lying prone upon the ground in the burning sun and greatly wounded by bursting shell and grapeshot.[4] His erect form and blazing eyes brought hope and courage to them in this their first baptism of fire.

At last, General Bee, seeing his thin ranks begin to waver, said, "General, they are beating us back." "Then," said Jackson, "we will give them the bayonet." Bee, catching the spirit of Jackson, galloped back to his men, saying, "There is Jackson, standing like a stone wall! Rally behind the Virginians!" A few score of the men rallied around the gallant Bee and charged upon the foe. In a few moments the same Bee fell dead with his face to the foe. "From that time," says Draper, a historian of the North, "the name which Jackson had received in a baptism of fire displaced that which he had received in a baptism of water, and he was known ever after as 'Stonewall Jackson.'"

Both of Jackson's flanks were now in danger and he saw that the moment had come to use the bayonet. Wheeling his cannon right and left, he gave the signal to his men to rise. He then cried out to the second regiment, "Reserve your fire until they come within fifty yards and then fire and give them the bayonet and, when you charge, yell like furies."

---

4.   A cluster of small iron balls fired from a cannon as a dispensing charge.

Rallying the Troops of Bee, Bartow, and Evans

His men sprang to their feet, fired one deadly volley, and then dashed down upon the foe. The latter could not stand this dreadful onset but turned and fled. A battery which had been captured by the foe was retaken and the center of the enemy's line of battle pierced by Jackson's men.

For four hours, Jackson had kept the enemy at bay but now help was nearby. Just as the Federals had rallied and again advanced in large numbers, General Kirby Smith, with a body of men which had come from the valley, and Generals Early and Holmes, with reserve troops, hurried up and struck the right wing of the Federal army while the Confederates in the center turned the Federal's own guns against them. This onset proved too much for the Federals. They again fired and, this time, their retreat became a general rout. The men in terror cast away their guns and, leaving cannons and flags, rushed for the nearest forts of Bull Run. The Confederate cavalry followed them while Kemper's field battery riddled them through and through with shells.

At once, the road to Washington became one surging mass of human beings struggling to escape the dreadful field of death. General Jackson's troops took no part in the pursuit except to plant a battery and to fire at the fleeing foe, many of whom did not stop until they were safe across the Long Bridge at Washington.

Though the Confederates were the victors, they had lost many brave men. Generals Bee and Bartow were killed and General Kirby Smith was badly wounded. General Jackson had been wounded in his left hand early in the action but had taken no notice of it. Now that the battle was over, he felt the pain acutely and went to the field hospital which had been placed by the side of a brook beneath the shade of some friendly willow trees.

When he came up, his friend Dr. McGuire said, "General, are you hurt much?" "No," replied he; "I believe it is a trifle." "How goes the day?" asked the Doctor, "Oh!" exclaimed Jackson, "We have beaten them; we have gained a glorious victory." Dr. Dabney says that this was the only time that Jackson was ever heard to express joy at having gained the day.

When the surgeons came around him to dress his wounded hand he said, "No, I can wait; my wound is but a trifle; attend first to those poor fellows." He then sat down upon the grass and waited until the wounds of the badly hurt had been dressed. At first, it was thought that his middle finger would have to be cut off, however, having been dressed very skillfully by Dr. McGuire, it was saved and his hand healed over time.

It is stated by several friends that General Jackson said, while having his hand dressed, that with ten thousand fresh troops he believed he could go into Washington City. As he was not the commanding general, however, he could not make the attempt but could only do as he was ordered.

I must not fail to give you a part of a letter which he wrote to his wife the day after the battle, July 22:

> Yesterday we fought a great battle and gained a great victory, for which all the glory is due *to God alone*. Though under fire for several hours, I received only one wound, the breaking of the longest finger of the left hand but the doctor says that it can be saved. My horse was wounded but not killed. My coat got an ugly wound near the hip…. While great credit is due to other parts of our gallant army, God made my brigade more instrumental than any other in repulsing the main attack.
>
> This is for you alone. Say nothing about it. Let another speak praise, not myself.

The praise of the Stonewall Brigade, however, was not sung by Jackson alone. Both friend and foe united in saying that if Jackson had not held the hill, which was the key to the Confederate position, until help came, the Battle of Manassas (Bull Run) would have been a defeat and not a victory for the South.

Jackson's eagle eye saw the place to make a stand and he held it for four hours against all odds.

Map of Eastern Virginia

Once while his men were lying upon the ground, they were so harassed by the bursting of shells that some officers begged to be permitted to advance. "No," said Jackson, "wait for the signal; this place must be held."

We do not seek to take glory from any other heroes of this extraordinary battle—many of whom, as Bee and Bartow, bravely gave up their lives in the storm of battle or, as Smith and Early, made forced marches to rescue those dreadfully pressed; but we do say, in one sense, that Jackson was the hero of the first battle of Manassas. In this battle, the Confederates captured twenty-eight cannons with five thousand muskets and vast stores of articles useful to their needy army.

The Confederates lost three hundred and sixty-nine killed on the field and fourteen hundred and eighty-three wounded.

The road to Washington was now open, for there is no doubt that General Jackson thought it best to press on while the enemy was routed and take possession of the city.

The commanding generals, however, were afraid to risk the attempt with an army which had been drilled only a few weeks and had so little discipline, thus the moment to strike passed by.

In a few days, the North had chosen a new commander, General George McClellan, who began to raise new armies to defend Washington and to scourge the South.

Soon after the battle, General Jackson moved his men to a piece of woodland nearby, where he employed the time in drilling his troops. After a time, the Confederate lines were pushed forward to within sight of Washington City

General George B. McClellan

but no battle took place as General McClellan was too wise to risk another engagement so soon after Manassas.

In October, General Jackson was promoted to the rank of major general and was sent to the Shenandoah Valley to take command of the army which had been fighting in West Virginia.

The Stonewall Brigade was left behind with General Johnston. This was a great trial, both to General Jackson and to the brigade. When the time came for him to leave for the new field of war, he ordered the brigade to march out under arms and then rode to the front with his staff. Dr. Dabney says that no cheer arose but every face was sad.

After speaking a few words of praise and love, he threw his bridle reins on the neck of his horse and, stretching his arms towards them, said:

In the Army of the Shenandoah, you were the First Brigade. In the Army of the Potomac, you were the First Brigade. In the Second Corps of the army, you are the First Brigade. You are the First Brigade in the affections of your General and, I hope by your future deeds and bearing, you will be handed down to posterity as the First Brigade in this, our second War of Independence. Farewell.

He then waved his hand and left the grounds at a gallop, followed by a few of his brave soldiers. This separation, however, was only for a short time. The following November, the First Brigade was ordered to join Jackson at Winchester and it remained with him until the fatal hour at Chancellorsville, when it lost him forever.

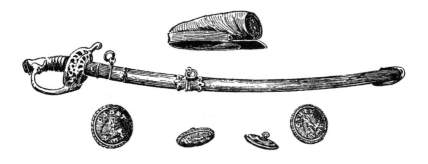

Chapter 7

A Gallant General

Spring 1862

When the year 1862 opened, General Jackson was at Winchester with ten thousand men. Generals Loring and Henry Jackson came from Western Virginia to join his command.

At the head of Jackson's cavalry was Lieutenant Colonel Ashby, a gallant, brave, and watchful officer. At the sound of his well known shout and the cry of "Ashby" from his men, the Federal soldiers would turn and flee as if from a multitude. Ever guarding the outposts of the army, he was Jackson's "eyes and ears."

Lieutenant Colonel Ashby

There were now three great armies threatening Jackson and he knew well that they would crush him if he did not meet each one before they could unite.

Jackson's little army was the guard to Johnston's flank. The latter general, with forty thousand men, was still at Manassas facing McClellan. McClellan, on the other hand, was at the head of an army of fifty thousand men and was preparing to "walk over Johnston" as soon as spring opened.

Jackson knew that if his army was defeated, Johnston would have to retreat and perhaps the whole State of Virginia would be given up to the foe. The armies were now in winter quarters and there was not much danger of a move before spring.

In the meantime, Jackson resolved to march against several large forces of Federals which were threatening him from the towns of Romney and Bath, forty miles away in northwestern Virginia.

It was the last of December, however, before he could collect the men and supplies necessary for the expedition. At last, on the first day of January 1862, all was ready. The little army of about nine thousand men set out without knowing if Jackson was leading, for he had not told even his officers his great plans.

In spite of the winter season, the day was bright and the air soft and balmy. So warm was the weather that the men left their overcoats and blankets to be brought on in the wagons. On the next day, a biting wind began to blow which was followed by rain and snow.

The men marched all day and at night the wagons, which had not been able to keep up with the troops, were still far behind. The troops rested that night without rations or blankets, having only campfires to keep off the cold.

On the third day, the men were so overcome by cold and hunger that they found it difficult to go forward. Jackson, riding grimly on the way, found his old brigade halted and asked General Garnett the reason for the delay.

"I have halted," said General Garrett, "to let the men cook rations."

"There is not time for it," replied General Jackson curtly.

"But it is impossible for the men to go farther without them," said General Garnett.

"I never found anything impossible with that brigade," said Jackson as he rode on.

He was certain that it was best to press forward; his plan to surprise the enemy would not work if his army delayed their march.

As the army neared the town of Bath, a force of Federals suddenly attacked it from behind trees and fences but it was soon driven off with the loss of twenty soldiers.

That night the Southern troops went into camp just outside the town, in the midst of a heavy snow storm. The men were without food or blankets and the amazing thing is how they lived through the night.

Jackson, however, did not change his plans, though there was great complaint among the men, many of whom straggled back to Winchester.

The next morning, after a hearty breakfast, the order was given to advance upon Bath. The artillery opened fire and the infantry charged the breastworks but the Federals hastily gave up the town and fled towards the Potomac River, which they waded that night.

The Southern troops, on entering the town, found quantities of stores which the Federals had left behind; among them were finer clothes, china, and even dinners, cooked and still smoking, ready to be eaten by the hungry Confederates.

From Bath, Jackson's men passed, with great difficulty and suffering, to a place called Hancock, about three miles away from Bath on the north side of the Potomac.

Jackson placed his cannons on the south bank and opened a hot fire on the town but the commander refused to surrender. As a large force of men came up to reinforce the Federals, Jackson decided to pass on to the city of Romney.

In the meantime, the railroad bridge over Capon River had been destroyed and the telegraph wires cut by General Loring so that the Union commander at Romney could not send for help.

The weather had now become terrible. Rain, snow, sleet, and hail beat down upon Jackson's men still without tents, overcoats, and blankets; for it was impossible for the wagons to come up. The mountain roads were covered with ice and sleet so that horses and men could not keep their footing. Many fell flat, badly hurt, while wagon after wagon slid down the steep banks and overturned.

Jackson was everywhere along the line cheering the troops and even helping them along. We are told by Cooke, our great Virginia writer, that, as Jackson was passing a point in the road where a piece of artillery had stalled and while a crowd of men were looking on without helping, he stopped, dismounted, and, without uttering a word, put his shoulder to the wheel. The men, shamed, came forward to take their places, the horses were whipped up and the piece moved on.

On January 14, after great hardships, the little army at last reached Romney to find that the Federals had retreated, leaving behind them large military stores which fell into the hands of the Confederates.

Even then, the name of Jackson was a terror to the foe. With a force much larger than Jackson's and when he was more than a day's march away, the Federals had fled. They left the greater part of their baggage and equipment.

In sixteen days, he had driven the enemy out of his district, had rendered the railroad useless to the Federals for more than a hundred miles, and had captured weapons enough to equip an army as large as his own. This he had done with the loss of four men killed and twenty-eight wounded.

Leaving General Loring at Romney with a portion of the army, Jackson hastened back to Winchester to watch the movements of General Banks who was stationed with a large Union army near Harpers Ferry.

Upon his return, he found the whole country in an uproar over the expedition to Romney through the sleet and snow. Though no one could say that Jackson was not full of courage and devotion to the South, many said that he was cruel and not fit to be in command of an army. Some said that he was a madman; others, that he was without common sense. Another charge against him was that he was partial to the Stonewall Brigade, as he had brought it back with him to the comforts of a town, while he had left Loring's command in the mountains. The soldiers of the brigade were called "Jackson's Pet Lambs" and other similar names. The truth was, however, that Loring's men were far more comfortable than those of the Stonewall Brigade; the former being ordered into huts, while the latter were in huts three miles from Winchester.

General Nathaniel P. Banks

Another charge against him was that he would tell his plans to no one. "It was his rule," says Dabney, "that in war, mystery was the key to success." He argued that no man could tell what bit of news might not be of use ᵗo the foe and therefore it was wisest to conceal everything.

This secrecy irritated his officers; and it must be said that some of them forgot their duty as soldiers to such an extent that they treated General Jackson with disrespect.

Though all of these charges were known to Jackson, he took no notice of them but proceeded to connect Romney with Winchester by telegraph wires. On January 31, however, he received this order from Richmond: "Order Loring back to Winchester at once."

The cause of this order was that some of the officers at Romney had sent a petition to Richmond asking to be sent back to Winchester, as the position at Romney was, in their opinion, too much exposed.

General Jackson obediently recalled the troops from Romney; nevertheless, he was so angry at the way in which he had been treated by the government that he at once resigned his command. This caused great excitement in the army and in the State at large. The people were by no means willing to give up an officer who had shown such courage and skill; therefore, they begged him to withdraw his resignation. This he refused to do. He said that the government had shown, by the order, that it did not trust him and that, if he was to be meddled with in that way, he could do no good. At last, however, a sort of an apology was made by the government, thus he quietly took up his duties again.

In a few days after General Loring left Romney, the Federals again took possession of that town and the country around. All the efforts of Jackson and the trials of his soldiers were thus undermined. This was a great blow to General Jackson, for Winchester was again exposed to the advance of the foe from four directions.

General Irvin McDowell

The plan for the invasion of Virginia in 1862 was almost the same as in 1861. Union General Fremont was marching from the northwest, Banks was coming from Harpers Ferry, while McDowell was advancing from Fredericksburg to face Johnston at Manassas. In addition, another large army under McClellan was at Fortress Monroe ready to march up the Peninsula.

The Northern army was much larger than the year before; the Southern army, however, was smaller since the active duty period of many of the men had expired and others had gone home on furlough. Several brigades were now taken from General Jackson to strengthen other points, thus he

The Union Army ready for Battle

found himself left with only six thousand men to guard the left flank of General Johnston's army and to protect the great Shenandoah Valley.

On February 26, Union General Banks, with thirty-five thousand men, and General Kelly, with eleven thousand, advanced against Jackson who was still at Winchester, hoping to hold that place until help could come from General Johnston.

As soon as Jackson found out through Colonel Ashby that he was almost surrounded by the enemy, he left Winchester and fell back slowly to Mt. Jackson, a village on the great turnpike, forty miles from Winchester. Here, he had sent all of his supplies and sick soldiers some weeks before. When the Federals entered Winchester, they found not a prisoner or a musket to "enrich their conquest."

It was a great trial to Jackson to leave his kind friends in Winchester but he promised them "he would wait for a better time and come again." We shall see how well he kept his promise.

On March 19, General Johnston wrote to General Jackson asking him to move closer to the enemy and to prevent him, if possible, from sending troops across to McClellan. Word was brought at the same time, that fifteen thousand men were marching with the army of Banks to help turn the left wing of Johnston's forces. The Confederate army, under Johnston, fell back to lines of defense nearer Richmond.

So Jackson gave orders to his little army, which now numbered only twenty-seven hundred men, to march back down the valley. That night the infantry slept at Strasburg, while Ashby's cavalry troops attacked the outposts of the Federals at Winchester.

"Beat the Rally!"

General Banks, thinking that Jackson would trouble him no more, had left for Washington and General Shields was in command of the Federal army in the valley.

On the morning of March 23, General Jackson pushed his whole force forward and, when about five miles from Winchester, he found Ashby fighting furiously with the advance of the foe at a place called Kernstown. Taking a good position, he at once joined the battle, though he saw that he was greatly out numbered. The battle raged from about noon until night. Regiment after regiment was hurled against Jackson's thin ranks but they fought stubbornly and would have gained the day had not the ammunition of the Stonewall Brigade given out.

Hearing his cannon fire dying away for lack of ammunition, General Garnett gave orders for his men to retreat. When Jackson saw the lines of his old brigade break apart, he galloped to the spot and, ordering Garnett to hold his ground, pushed forward to rally the men. Seeing a drummer boy retreating like the rest, he seized him by the shoulder, dragged him in full view of the soldiers, and said in his sternest tones, "Beat the rally!" The drummer beat the rally and in the midst of a storm of balls Jackson saw the lines reform.

It was too late, however. The enemy now pressed forward in such numbers that there was nothing left to do but to retreat. This they did in good order but the Northern troops held the field of battle where numerous dead and wounded men were lying.

In this Battle of Kernstown twenty-seven hundred Confederates, with eleven guns, attacked eleven thousand Federals and almost gained the victory. It is said that General Shields had just given orders for his men to retreat when the Stonewall Brigade fell back.

As General Shields followed Jackson up the Valley after the battle, he stopped at a noted country house for the night. General Jackson had also rested there upon his retreat and, from his adjutant,[5] the lady of the house had learned the correct number of Jackson's men.

General Shields, at breakfast, entered into a conversation with his hostess and in a polite way boasted of his great victory.

---

5. A military staff officer who serves as an administrative assistant to the commanding officer.

"Ah! General," said the lady, "We can afford such defeats as that, when twenty-seven hundred men hold back eleven thousand for hours and then retreat at leisure! Such defeats are victories." General Shields was surprised to learn the small number of Jackson's forces and begged the lady to tell him her informant. "Certainly," said the lady, "General Jackson's adjutant, Major Paxton. I have also information that large reinforcements are coming to Jackson and that he will again be ready to meet you." "I have no doubt of that, my dear Madam," stated the Union General.

Major E. F. Paxton

That night Jackson's little army rested near Newtown while Ashby kept watch not far from the field of battle. "Jackson," says Cooke, "got an armful of corn for his horse and, wrapping his blanket about him, lay down by a fire in a fence corner and went to sleep." Though defeated for the first and last time, he had won the object of the battle. The fifteen thousand men who had started across the mountains to McClellan were recalled to the Valley and Johnston was able to move safely behind the Rappahannock River, his new line of defense.

At four o'clock on the morning of March 24, Jackson began to retreat slowly and in good order. The enemy pursued for awhile but at last fell back to Winchester.

Jackson's army was far from cast down by the defeat at Kernstown. The soldiers felt that they had made a splendid fight against three times their number. Now, too, for the first time, it began to dawn upon them that their general was a great leader. As Jackson passed among the columns, the men would cheer themselves hoarse.

Cooke tells us that one man was heard to ask, as he struggled along, "Why is Old Jack a better general than Moses?" "Because it took Moses forty years to lead the Israelites through the wilderness and Old Jack would have double-quicked them through it in three days!"

It is said by another writer, that the men would laugh and say that the only rest they had was when they were retreating before the enemy. He always led them by forced marches when going to attack the foe but never fast enough on a retreat to miss the chance of a fight.

The weather was now mild and balmy and the men suffered few hardships during their slow retreat. At last they reached the old camp at Mt. Jackson where Jackson gathered up his wounded and sent them up the valley.

On the first of April, he crossed the north fork of the Shenandoah and took position on Rude's Hill, five miles below the town of New Market.

General Banks had again come up the valley and was pressing upon the rear of Jackson's army.

It was necessary for Colonel Ashby to burn the bridge near Mt. Jackson, after the Southern army had passed over. While Ashby and his men were engaged in this work, the Federal cavalry dashed up and a skirmish ensued in which Ashby's beautiful snow white horse was mortally wounded.

General Jackson remained at Rude's Hill until the waters so subsided that the Northern army could cross the river. On April 17, he again took up his line of march through New Market to Harrisonburg.

At the last named place, he turned east and, passing the south end of Massanutton Mountain, crossed the south branch of the

Shenandoah River and posted his troops in the gorge of the Blue Ridge called Swift Run Gap.

JACKSON'S MARCH
May~June 1862

The way to Staunton was now open to General Banks and his troops but he was too timid to go forward. Jackson in his back was worse than Jackson in front of him. For two weeks, Jackson held the Gap while Banks occupied Harrisonburg and laid waste to the country.

Jackson now had about eight thousand men and thirty guns. His men had returned from hospitals and furloughs and a number of new recruits had also joined to help in this time of danger. The General employed these weeks of rest in organizing and drilling his men and in mending up his old artillery. In the meantime, he also made bold plans and, with the help of General Robert E. Lee, who had now been made commander of the "Army of Northern Virginia," proceeded to carry them out.

In order to understand the great genius of our hero and the bravery and endurance of his men, study the map on the next page.

You will see that the valley of the Shenandoah is bounded on the east by the Blue Ridge Mountains and on the west by the Alleghany. Winchester is situated in the northern part of the Valley, while Staunton is about ninety miles to the south. These two places are connected by a fine turnpike.

Near the center of the valley, rises a beautiful mountain which the Indians called Massanutton and which still retains that name.

This mountain begins near Strasburg and extends about fifty miles towards Staunton, ending abruptly not far from Harrisonburg.

There is only one gap in the Massanutton Mountain and that is opposite the towns of New Market and Luray.

The valley east of the mountain is called the Page Valley, while the entire valley, including the Page Valley, is part of the Shenandoah Valley.

Some of the young people who will read this book live under the shadow and in the sight of this lovely mountain, which enabled Jackson to play "hide and seek" with his foe. Hopefully, they will understand thoroughly the great movements which ensue.

Though Jackson and his little army were safe for awhile in Swift Run Gap—opposite the village of Elkton, they could not have remained there long since three major generals, with as many large armies, were marching to surround and crush them. Banks was only fifteen miles away, Milroy was coming by way of Staunton from western Virginia, and Fremont was advancing from the northwest. At Fredericksburg, General McDowell was also ordered to send twenty thousand men to the valley, instead of advancing to help McClellan, who was now near Richmond with a large army. In essence, Jackson was bravely obeying General Johnston's orders to keep the Northern armies busy in the valley to prevent them from reinforcing McClellan.

There was now a small force of Confederates under General Edward Johnson on Shenandoah Mountain, twenty miles west of Staunton. There was great danger that Milroy, with his larger army, would overcome Johnson, take Staunton, and march on to join Banks. Their two armies would then be large enough to crush Jackson.

It was also important to keep the city of Staunton out of the hands of the foe, as it was situated on the Chesapeake and Ohio railway, which carried supplies from the fertile valley to Richmond.

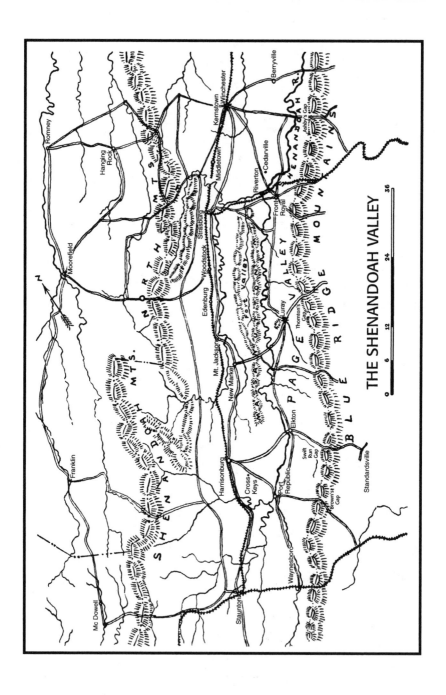

THE SHENANDOAH VALLEY

General Jackson, therefore, wrote to General Lee that he would go to the aid of Johnson and protect Staunton, if Lee would send a force to hold Banks in check during his absence.

This General Lee did, sending from Richmond General Ewell (u-el)—a brave officer, with eight thousand men, who marched into Swift Run Gap from the east and took the places which Jackson's men had just left.

It was now Jackson's object to reach the city of Staunton without the knowledge of General Banks, thus he marched, with great difficulty, through miry roads and

General Richard S. Ewell

down the mountain about eight miles to another gap across the Blue Ridge, called Brown's Gap. When there, he turned east and marched swiftly across the mountain into Albemarle County, passing though the village of White Hall to Mechum's River Station. The troops then were carried swiftly by rail to Staunton, reaching there the night of May 4, to the great joy of the people of Staunton who thought that they had been deserted by Jackson in their time of need.

By Monday, the whole army had come up. They were then joined by General Johnson and his army. On May 7, one day having been spent in preparing for the march, Jackson, with General Johnson's command in front, marched towards Milroy, who was now posted on Shenandoah Mountain.

Jackson had been joined at Staunton by the corps of cadets from the Military Institute at Lexington under Col. Scott Shipp. Many of them were mere boys but they were filled with joy at taking their first look at grim war under Stonewall Jackson, who had been a professor in their school before the war.

As the Confederate army approached Shenandoah Mountain, the Northern troops retreated to the village of McDowell.

On Thursday, May 8, Jackson and Johnson, with the command of the latter still in advance, climbed the sides of the mountain overlooking that little village.

That evening, while the generals were waiting for the rest of the army to come up, Northern troops under General Milroy made an attack upon their position. Though not expecting an attack, Jackson quickly placed his troops for the conflict—the center of the line being held by the Twelfth Georgia regiment with great bravery. Once it was related that, when ordered to retire behind the crest of the hill to escape the raking fire of the foe, they refused to evacuate and kept their position. The next day, a tall youth from the Georgia regiment was asked why they did not fall back as ordered. He replied, "We did not come all the way to Virginia to run before Yankees."

Just before the close of the battle, General Johnson was wounded in the ankle and compelled to leave the field.

The Battle of McDowell raged from 4:30 to 8:30 P.M., the shades of night closing the conflict. Then the Federals gave up the assault and retreated from the field. "By nine o'clock," says Dr. Dabney, "the roar of the struggle had passed away and the green battlefield reposed under the starlight as calmly as when it had been occupied only by its peaceful herds of cattle."

It was 1:00 A.M. before General Jackson reached his tent, having waited to see the last wounded man brought off the battlefield and the last picket[6] posted. He had eaten nothing since morning but, when his faithful servant Jim came with food, he said, "I want none, nothing but sleep," and in a moment he was fast asleep.

General Jackson was in the saddle at the break of day. Upon climbing the mountain, however, he saw that the enemy had left during the night. He at once sent this dispatch to Richmond: "God blessed our arms with victory at McDowell yesterday." He then set out in pursuit of the fleeing Federals. He had followed them as far as Franklin when the woods were set on fire by the Federals to conceal their position.

The dense smoke hung like a dark, gloomy covering over the mountain roads and the heat from the blazing forests was terrible. The long column, however, pressed on until Monday when General Jackson received an order from General Lee to return to the Valley and "pay his respects" to General Banks who was now at Strasburg.

Time was now precious to Jackson. After halting for a brief rest—during which time the whole army met to render thanks to God for the great victory, he set out on his return march to the Valley.

On May 20, he was again in the city of New Market where he was joined by General Ewell. By a bold plan and a swift march, he had saved the army of General Johnson and prevented Milroy from capturing the city of Staunton and joining Banks. After this achievement, Jackson was again in pursuit of the Federal army commanded by Banks. General Banks was fortifying at the city of Strasburg and seemed to expect an attack in front, therefore, Jackson wisely planned to attack him in the rear.

You remember that I told you that just east of New Market there is a pass, or gap, through the Massanutton Mountain. Now Jackson sent a small force of cavalry down the turnpike towards Strasburg to

---

6. A soldier stationed at an outpost or on a line forward of where the main body of troops are positioned, to warn the troops of an enemy advance; lookouts or scouts.

The Twelfth Georgia Regiment at McDowell

hold it and conceal the movements of the main army which he himself led eastward across the mountain into the Page Valley.

Hidden by the friendly mountain, his troops marched quickly and silently to the town of Front Royal, which is at the northern end of the mountain and which then guarded the flank of Bank's army.

So swift and silent had been the march that Jackson's men were nearly in sight of the town before anyone knew of their presence. One mile and a half from the town, the Federal pickets were driven in and an instant advance was ordered. The Confederate troops rushed to the attack. The Federals, thinking that Jackson was at least one hundred miles away in the mountains of Western Virginia, were taken completely by surprise. They surrendered by hundreds, giving up quantities of valuable stores, among which were five hundred new revolvers and a wagon load of coffee.

The people of Front Royal were wild with joy at seeing the Confederates again but the troops were not permitted to stop. On through the town they went at double-quick, for the Federals had now made a stand outside of the town. The Federal troops, however, were speedily put to flight and the pursuit went on.

In the meantime, the Confederate cavalry came upon a body of Federals near Cedarville, five miles from Front Royal. A charge was at once made upon the Federals by the Confederates and the whole force was driven back. The Federals then reformed in an orchard and were again charged upon by the Confederates. After a fierce contest, however, they were captured.

As night came on, the weary Southern troops went into camp, for they were quite worn out with marching and fighting.

The next morning, May 24, the troops were again moving by the break of day. Our hero himself rode forward towards Middletown. When in sight of the turnpike which leads from Strasburg to Winchester, he saw long lines of Federal horsemen in full retreat.

The batteries of Poague and Chew were brought forward and a hot fire opened upon the retreating foe. The latter broke in wild confusion and soon the turnpike was filled with a mass of struggling and dying horses and men. A few regiments which formed the rear guard fell back to Strasburg and, leaving their baggage at that place, fled through the western mountains to the Potomac River.

Jackson's Troops on the Move Again

On the turnpike, Ashby with his cavalry followed closely after the fleeing foe, firing upon them with shot and shell. Cooke says:

> Either a shell or a round of shot would strike one of the wagons and overturn it and, before those behind could stop their headway, they would thunder down on the remains of the first. Others would tumble in so as to block up the road and, in the midst of it all, Ashby's troopers would swoop down taking prisoners or cutting down such as resisted.

Ashby himself pressed forward and, at one time, it is said, took as many as thirty prisoners, unaided and alone.

But Ashby's men soon began to plunder the wagons, which were rich in supplies and thus gave the enemy time to recover from their panic. When near Newtown, the enemy turned and fired upon their pursuers. At dark, however, the firing ceased and Jackson himself went forward to urge on the pursuit.

The main body of the army had now come up, however, no halt was made for food or rest. The so-called "foot cavalry" of the valley marched all night along the pike lit up by "burning wagons, pontoon bridges, and lanterns."

Every now and then, they would come upon men hidden along the sides of the road and fierce fights would ensue.

About dawn on May 25, Jackson's advanced force climbed the lofty hill southwest of Winchester. This hill was already held by the Federals; however, they were charged upon by the Stonewall Brigade and driven back. With a loud shout, the Confederates gained the crest of the hill and planted their batteries. Though they had marched all night, they took no rest or food but at once began the Battle of Winchester.

Ewell fought on the right and Taylor on the left. "Jackson," says a writer, "had his 'war look' on and rode about the field, regardless of shot and shell, looking as calm as if nothing was going on."

At last, after a fierce fight, the Federals gave way and Jackson entered Winchester at the heels of the panic-stricken Union army. The people of the town were beside themselves with delight to see their beloved general once more. Jackson was for the first time excited. He waved his faded cap around his head and cheered with a right good will.

The troops, however, still pressed forward—Jackson leading the way. When one of his officers said, "Don't you think you are going into too much danger, General?" his reply was, "Tell the troops to press right on to the Potomac." They *did* press onward until the enemy was forced across the Potomac River with the loss of many prisoners and valuable equipment.

After resting a few days, Jackson advanced towards Harpers Ferry with the view of attacking the Federal force there. He was stopped, however, by the news that two armies—one under General Shields from the east, the other under General Fremont from the west—were to cut him off on the way and capture him.

He at once hastened back to Winchester where he collected his prisoners and the stores of ammunition and medicine which he had captured. These he sent up the valley and followed rapidly with his whole army.

In the meantime, there was great terror at Washington, the Union capital, and in the North. Men wore anxious faces and were asking each other, "Where is Jackson?" They were afraid that he would turn and capture Washington.

Jackson, however, had only about fifteen thousand men and could not risk the loss of the rich stores which he had gained and the destruction of his noble army; thus he put forth all his skill and nerve to save them.

The Confederates now began a race to reach Strasburg before the Federals. The larger part of the army marched from near Harpers Ferry to Strasburg, nearly fifty miles, in about twenty-four hours. This rapid advance confirms why Jackson's troops might well be called the "foot cavalry."

As Jackson marched into Strasburg, General Fremont's advance was almost in sight and, as the Stonewall Brigade had not yet come up, Jackson sent General Ewell to hold Fremont in check. A fierce battle ensued but Ewell at last drove back the enemy. The Stonewall Brigade came up that evening and the whole army continued to move up the valley.

The race had been won by Jackson who was safe for the present. In a brief space of time, he had flanked the enemy at Front Royal, chased them to Middletown, beaten them at Winchester, and sent them flying across the Potomac River. When nearly entrapped by two other columns, he had passed between them and was now hurrying with his rich supplies to the upper valley. Cooke tells us that he had captured two thousand three hundred prisoners, one hundred cattle, thirty-four thousand pounds of bacon, salt, sugar, coffee, hard bread, and cheese, valuable medical stores, $125,185 worth of other stores, two pieces of artillery, and many small arms and horses. All this was gained with the loss of about four hundred men.

As Jackson retreated up the valley, he was again threatened by a great danger. Shields's column marched up the Page Valley with the view of crossing the Massanutton Mountain at New Market and striking Jackson from the rear, just as Jackson had done to Banks when he went down to Front Royal. Jackson, however, was too wary to be taken by surprise.

He sent swift horsemen across the mountain and over the south branch of the Shenandoah to burn the White House and Columbia Mills bridges, thus preventing Shields from executing his plans. In addition, they placed signal stations on top of the mountain to inform him of what was going on in the Page Valley.

Fremont was now pressing at Jackson's rear guard; nevertheless, he moved swiftly up the valley with his main army while Ashby kept guard on every side. When Harrisonburg was reached, he again marched east and took his stand near the village of Port Republic.

On the sixth of June, as the gallant Ashby was leading a charge to repel the advance of the Federal forces, he fell—pierced to the heart by a single bullet. His last words were, "Charge Virginians!" Thus, in the moment of victory, the brave and noble Ashby died. His loss was deeply felt by Jackson who now, more than ever, needed the daring and skill of his "Chief of Cavalry."

Jackson stood his ground at Port Republic, a village at the forks of the Shenandoah River. Fremont was at Harrisonburg, fifteen miles to the northwest on the west side of the river, and Shields was at Conrad's Store, fifteen miles to the northeast on the east side of the river. The space between the three generals formed the sides of a triangle. Just behind Jackson, in the Blue Ridge Mountains, was

Brown's Gap, through which he could retreat and join Lee near the town of Richmond.

Jackson had no intent of leaving the valley without a parting blow. The Shenandoah was so high that Shields and Fremont could not unite their forces. Jackson therefore determined to attack Shields first and, if victorious, then to turn his attention to Fremont. Over the north branch between Jackson and Fremont there was a bridge but over the south branch between Jackson and Shields there was only a stream. The north bank was high, while the south was low and stretched away in broad meadows towards the mountains.

Jackson, leaving the trusty Ewell at Cross Keys to watch Fremont, took possession of the heights overlooking the bridge at Port Republic and stationed there two brigades and his remaining artillery. A small body of cavalry was sent across South River to find out the position of Shields.

Early on the morning of June 8, the cavalry came galloping back with the news that Shield's army was close at hand. Jackson, who was in the town with some of his staff, at once gave orders for the batteries on the north side to open fire but before it could be done, the Federal cavalry dashed into the town followed by artillery which rumbled forward and took position at the southern end of the bridge.

Jackson and his staff were now cut off from his army which was on the north bank. We are told by the historian Cooke and others that Jackson, with great presence of mind, rode towards the bridge and, rising in his stirrups, called sternly to the Federal officer commanding the gun: "Who told you to post that gun there, sir? Bring it over here!" The officer, thinking that Jackson was a Federal general, bowed, "limbered up" the piece, and was preparing to move. In the meantime, Jackson and his staff galloped across the bridge and were soon safe on the northern side.

No time was lost by the Confederates. Their artillery opened fire upon the Federals and Jackson himself led the Thirty-seventh Virginia regiment, drove the foe from the bridge, and captured the gun with the loss of only two men wounded.

Meanwhile, Jackson's long wagon train, which contained his ammunition, was bravely defended on the outskirts of the village by a handful of pickets and a section of artillery until help came.

The fire of the guns on the north bank made it impossible for the Federals to hold the village. Leaving their other gun, they retreated and dashed across the stream of the South River by the way they had come.

Hardly had the guns stopped firing at Port Republic, before heavy firing was heard in the direction of Cross Keys, five miles off. The noise came from fighting between Ewell and Fremont. The latter had twenty thousand men, while General Ewell had only about six thousand. The Confederates were posted with great skill upon a ridge and, after fighting from 10:00 A.M. until nightfall, at last drove back the enemy with great loss. The Battle of Cross Keys having been fought, the Confederate troops lay upon their arms, only to renew the battle the next day.

Jackson, however, had other plans. He had determined to strike Shields next. Leaving a guard to watch General Fremont, he ordered Ewell to march at break of day to Port Republic.

At midnight he caused a footbridge to be thrown across South River so that his infantry might pass over to attack Shields. This bridge was made by placing wagons lengthwise across the swollen stream. The floor of the bridge was formed of long boards laid loosely from one wagon to another. Over this rude, frail structure, the whole body of infantry passed but not as quickly as its general wished. For some reason, about halfway across the stream, one wagon was about two feet higher than the others thus making a step. All the boards on the higher wagon, however, were not tight.

General Jackson at Port Republic Bridge

When the column began to cross over, several men were thrown by
the loose planks into the water; therefore, refusing to trust anything

but the firm planks, the men went, at this point, in single file. This made the crossing very tedious and, instead of being in line to attack Shields at sunrise, it was ten o'clock before the entire army had passed over.

Those loose boards cost the Confederates a bloody battle, for they found the Federals drawn up in battle array and ready for the fight. This incident shows how much care should be taken in performing the most trivial duty, as the success of great events is often affected by very slight causes. It is reported that Jackson hoped to surprise General Shields, whip him in a few hours, and then recross the river to rout Fremont.

The Battle of Port Republic on June 9, however, raged furiously for hours. The Union troops fought with great courage and it was not until evening that they gave way and retreated from the field. The Confederates followed them eight or nine miles down the river and returned laden with spoils and prisoners.

At ten o'clock in the morning, Jackson sent orders for the guard left at Cross Keys under General Trimble and Colonel Patton to march to his aid and to burn the bridge behind them. This they did and came up in time to join in the fight.

Towards nightfall General Jackson led his weary troops by a side road into the safe recesses of Brown's Gap in the Blue Ridge Mountains. As they passed the field of battle on their return, they saw the hills on the north side of the river crowded with the Union troops of General Fremont, who had arrived in time to see the rout of Shields.

The river being high, they did not attempt to cross but began a furious cannonade upon the Confederate surgeons and men who were caring for the wounded and burying the dead.

The next day, scouts brought word to Jackson that Fremont was building a bridge but soon after he retreated, having undoubtedly learned that General Shields's army was entirely routed.

On June 12, the Confederate cavalry under Colonel Munford entered Harrisonburg. Fremont traveled back down the valley, leaving behind him his sick and wounded and many valuable supplies. Four hundred and fifty Federals were taken prisoner on the field, while as many more were found in the hospitals. One thousand small arms and nine field pieces fell to the victorious Confederates. The Federal loss in the two battles was about two thousand. In the Battle of Cross Keys, Jackson lost only forty-two killed and two hundred and thirty-one wounded but in the Battle of Port Republic, ninety-one officers and men were killed and six hundred and eighty-six wounded.

Though Jackson's plans had not been entirely carried out, he was now rid of the two armies of forty thousand men which had been on his front and flanks and had threatened to crush him.

Within forty days his troops had marched four hundred miles, fought four great battles, and defeated four separate armies, sending to the rear over three thousand prisoners and vast trains of stores and ammunition.

From this time, Jackson stood forth as a leader of great genius; the little orphan boy had indeed climbed the heights of fame amid a "blaze of glory."

On the twelfth of June, Jackson led his army from its camp in Brown's Gap to the plains of Mt. Meridian, a few miles above Port Republic. Here, the wearied men rested for five days while Colonel Munford, who now commanded the cavalry, kept watch on the turnpike below Harrisonburg.

This is the dispatch which Jackson sent to Richmond:

Near Port Republic, June 9, 1862.

Through God's blessing, the enemy near Port Republic was this day routed with the loss of six pieces of his artillery.

T. J. JACKSON
Major General, Commanding

The Saturday following the battle was set apart by General Jackson as a day of thanksgiving and prayer and on Sunday the Lord's Supper was celebrated by the Christian soldiers from all the army. General Jackson was present at this service and partook of the sacred feast in company with his men.

On June 16, General Jackson ordered Colonel Munford to press down the pike, if possible, as far as New Market, making the enemy believe that his whole army was advancing. Colonel Munford succeeded and the Federals, believing that Jackson was again on the march, retreated to Strasburg and began to fortify themselves.

Meanwhile, on June 17, Jackson had begun a march but not towards Strasburg. The mighty army of George McClellan had advanced so close to Richmond that at night the reflection of its camp fires could be seen from the city and General Lee sent for Jackson to come to his aid as swiftly as possible.

Great care was taken to make the Federals believe that troops were being sent to Jackson. In this way, he could again go down the Valley and attack Fremont and Shields at Strasburg. A division of men was sent as far as Staunton and the report was spread that a large force was on the march to Jackson. The truth was, however, that our hero was already on his way to Richmond where the next blow was to be struck.

It was important to keep the Northern Generals in ignorance of Jackson's movement. Colonel Munford was thus ordered to make a great show with his men along the turnpike and to allow no news to be carried to the foe. The men were told to give this answer to all questions, "I do not know." The historian Cooke tells us this amusing incident which grew out of the above order. "One of Hood's men left the ranks to go to a cherry tree nearby, when Jackson rode past and saw him. 'Where are you going?' asked the General. 'I don't know,' replied the soldier. 'To what command do you belong?' 'I don't know.' 'Well, what State are you from?' 'I don't know.' 'What is the meaning of all this?' asked Jackson. 'Well,' was the reply, 'Old Stonewall and General Hood issued orders yesterday that we were not to know anything until after the next fight.' Jackson laughed and rode on."

On June 25, the corps reached Ashland near Richmond.

Jackson had gone on in advance to the headquarters of General Lee where his post in the coming strife was assigned him.

Confederate Battery

Chapter 8

A Major General

Summer 1862

General McClellan was now on the banks of the Chickahominy River, at one point only six miles from Richmond, with the largest and best equipped army that had ever been raised upon American soil.

His position was a strong one, having the Pamunkey River on one side and the James on the other, with the marshes of the Chickahominy in front as natural barriers to the assaults of the Confederates. Besides, he had thoroughly fortified his line which swept in a crescent shape from Meadow Bridge Road on the right, across the Chickahominy, to the Williamsburg Road on the left—a distance of about fifteen miles.

General Ambrose Powell Hill

General Lee now determined to send General Jackson to the rear of the enemy to turn their flank. At the same time, Generals A. P. Hill and Longstreet would attack them in front.

On the evening of June 26, General A. P. Hill advanced upon Mechanicsville and attacked the strong position of the Federals. The latter defended themselves bravely but at last fell back to their works on Beaverdam Creek. The victorious Confederates followed and an artillery fire was sustained until nine o'clock at night. The attack was renewed at dawn the next morning and raged for hours—when suddenly the Federals retreated in haste from their strong position, leaving everything in flames.

Jackson had come up, turned their flank, and caused them to retire. Generals Hill and Longstreet followed them until about noon. At once, they found the Federals again drawn up for battle behind Powhite Creek on a ridge whose slope was fortified by breastworks of trees and whose crest was crowned with batteries of frowning guns.

The Confederate troops immediately advanced but were repulsed with great loss. Again, they charged up the hill and gained the crest only to be driven back by the storm of shot and shell.

Longstreet was now ordered to make a move on the right towards Gaines's Mill where the Federals were massed in a strong position. In the meantime, General Lee ordered General Jackson to advance to the help of General Hill. About five o'clock in the evening, the sound of guns was heard to the left and soon Jackson's corps was in the thickest of the fight.

Before them lay a swamp, a deep stream, masses of felled timber, a wood filled with armed men, and cannons belching forth shot and shell. The work was hard but, when Jackson gave the order, his men swept forward with wild cheers and a roar of musketry, while above the clang arose the cry of "Jackson! Jackson! Jackson!"

The men rushed on through the swamp, across the creek, and up into the wood and drove the enemy from point to point until they gained the top of the hill.

On the right of the line, Hood's Texas brigade charged with a yell, leaped ditch and stream, and drove the foe pell-mell before them. In this charge, they lost one thousand men but took fourteen cannons and nearly a regiment of prisoners.

The enemy now retreated in wild disorder all along the line and the Battle of Old Cold Harbor was won by the Confederates. The very name of Jackson struck terror to the foe!

The next morning, June 29, Jackson was ordered to move on the rear of McClellan's army.

At Savage Station, the Confederates under General Magruder had a fierce fight with the rear guard of the Federals. At nightfall the latter again gave way, leaving behind equipment and several wounded men. While the battle at Savage Station had been going on, the main body of the Federal army passed over the bridge at White Oak swamp and destroyed it. For the time being, they were safe because the Confederates could not pass over the marshy stream under the fire of the Federals, who were massed on the opposite bank.

General John B. Hood

General Jackson opened fire with his artillery and, the next morning, July 1, forced the passage of White Oak swamp and captured a part of the Federal artillery.

Meanwhile, a fierce battle had been fought at Frasier's farm by Generals Longstreet and A. P. Hill with another part of McClellan's army. Under cover of night, the Union soldiers decided to move on, leaving their dead and wounded and many prisoners.

General Jackson was now placed in front of the Confederate forces in pursuit of the foe, who was nearing the James River. It was General Lee's plan to cut them off from the river and destroy the whole army; however, the Confederates were worn out by hard fighting and General McClellan was allowed to make a stand on Malvern Hill. He hastily fortified this strong position and, like a wild animal at bay, his whole army was determined to contend for their existence.

General Lee ordered an assault, placing Jackson and D. H. Hill on the left and Magruder on the right. Owing to the timber and marshes, the Confederates could use but little artillery while the Federals, from their greater height, rained a storm of shot and shell from three hundred cannons. The gunboats on the James also threw their monstrous shells above the heads of the Confederates. Despite all odds, Jackson's devoted men charged across the marshes and up the hill, forcing the enemy back. After a fierce combat, however, they fell back with great loss. Again and again they charged with the same result. At sunset, Magruder, who with much difficulty had gotten his troops into position, charged on the right with great bravery.

General McClellan's Pontoon Bridge across the James River

As darkness came on, the Confederates fought with renewed courage. Whole lines of the enemy fell beneath their musket fire but the Federal guns could not be taken by the Confederates since no line of men could live within the zone of fire which flamed from the mouths of the blazing cannons.

About ten o'clock at night, the firing stopped and the Confederate troops, holding their position, slept upon the battlefield.

When the battle had ended, Jackson went slowly to the rear where his faithful servant Jim was waiting for him with food and a pallet made upon the ground. After eating a few morsels, Jackson lay down and fell into a deep sleep. About one o'clock in the morning, Generals Hill, Ewell, and Early came to tell him that their commands were cut to pieces and that they would not be able to continue the fight when day broke. Jackson listened to them in silence and then said: "McClellan and his army will be gone by daylight." The generals thought he was crazy but, when morning came, they found that he had correctly predicted the flight of McClellan. Malvern Hill was found to be deserted by the foe. The Union army had retreated during the night to Harrison's landing under cover of their gunboats and Richmond was for the time safe.

The Battle of Malvern Hill was a dearly bought victory for the Confederates. In the battle, General Jackson lost three hundred and seventy-seven men killed and one thousand seven hundred and forty-six wounded, with thirty-nine missing. As soon as possible, the Southern army followed McClellan but found him too strongly entrenched to attack. The worn out men, therefore, went into camp nearby and retreated for the first time in a fortnight.

General Jackson soon grew weary of watching McClellan and began to plan a bold march into Maryland to threaten Washington City. It was not long before he did move northward. News came that a Union army of forty thousand men, under General Pope, was coming towards Gordonsville to the help of McClellan. General Jackson was immediately ordered to advance to meet him and drive him back.

General Jackson Preparing for Battle

His corps moved forward and, on August 9, fought the Battle of Cedar Run. In this fierce battle, one of the regiments began to fall back. At that instant, Jackson placed himself in front of his men, drew his sword, and cried in a voice of thunder, "Rally, brave men! Jackson will lead you! Follow me!" This turned the tide of battle and the Federal army broke into full retreat. Just before this battle, some officers inquired of Jim, the General's servant, if there were any signs of a battle. "Oh, yes, sir," replied he, "the General is a great man for praying night and morning; all times, but when I see him get up in the night and go off to pray, then I know there is going to be an important battle and I go right straight and pack his haversack, for I know he will call for it in the morning."

General Lee now came up with the greater part of the Southern army, leaving only a small force to watch General McClellan. The plan of the Southern leaders was to rout General Pope and march northward to threaten Washington, compelling General McClellan to leave his camp on the James River.

The main body of Lee's army moved nearer to Pope's front while Jackson's corps moved off to the northwest and was again "lost." It was marching across the Rappahannock and behind the Bull Run Mountains which hid it from the enemy.

On August 26, it passed through the mountains at Thoroughfare Gap and took position between General Pope and Washington City.

Jackson at once took Manassas Junction, where three hundred prisoners and immense quantities of stores were captured. The poor, hungry soldiers took what could be carried away and the rest was burned.

When Pope heard that Jackson was at his rear, he moved to meet him and ordered McDowell to close in upon him from the direction of Gainesville, saying, "We shall bag the whole crowd." The wary Jackson, however, was a match for his foes. Taking a good position upon the old battlefield of Manassas, he at once attacked the enemy coming up on the evening of August 28. When darkness fell upon the blood-drenched plain, the Confederates were the victors. On the next morning, the fight was renewed but Jackson's men were almost exhausted, when Longstreet's corps appeared and soon turned the tide of battle.

It was not long before Pope's army was in full retreat towards Washington and Jackson was again the victor. During a part of the battle, a severe storm came up. An aide from General A.P. Hill rode up and reported that his ammunition was wet and asked leave to retire. "Give my compliments to General Hill," said Jackson, "and tell him that the Yankee ammunition is as wet as his and to stay where he is." "There was always blood and danger," says a friend, "when Jackson began his sentences with 'Give my compliments.'"

General Lee now determined to cross the Potomac and threaten Washington and Jackson led the advance. On September 6, he reached Frederick and remained there several days, resting and refitting his command. On September 10, when General Lee came up, he at once sent General Jackson to Harpers Ferry to capture the Federal forces there. After taking the heights around town, he proceeded to take the town by storm.

In a short while the garrison of eleven thousand men, with seventy-three cannons, thirteen thousand rifles and a vast amount of stores, surrendered. Jackson, leaving General Hill to receive the captured prisoners and property, immediately set out to return to General Lee at Sharpsburg, a little

Burnside's Bridge Attack

village two and one-half miles from the Potomac River. After a weary night march, he reached that place on the morning of September 16. He found General Lee facing the hosts of McClellan and drawn up for battle. When he had released his worn out men for several hours, he took his position on the left, next to the Potomac River. This was the post of danger, for against it McClellan massed forty-four thousand men on September 17.

After extreme fighting and marching, the corps of Jackson now numbered less than seven thousand men. This little band, however, held the ground throughout the day and bravely drove back every assault of the enemy.

When night closed the bloody fray, each army held its own position. On the next morning, General Lee awaited another attack but General McClellan had received so heavy a blow that he would not venture another battle until fresh troops had come up.

September 18 was spent by both armies in burying their dead and caring for the wounded. In the evening, General Lee, learning that large bodies of fresh troops were reaching McClellan, determined to recross the Potomac. When night came, the troops began to move towards the fort at Shepherdstown. "For hours," says Dr. Dabney, "Jackson was seen seated upon his horse, motionless as a statue, watching the passage until the last man and the last carriage had touched the Southern shore." The Battle of Sharpsburg, or Antietam (An te´tam) as it is sometimes called, was a drawn battle. Neither side was victorious, each losing in killed and wounded about twelve thousand men. This short battle was the most bloody engagement of the entire war. Entire regiments on both sides were almost completely wiped out.

The southern men were so worn out and footsore from the constant marching and weak from starvation that they were really unfit for the Battle of Sharpsburg. More than half of Lee's army was left behind along the Virginia roads and those who fought the battle

Stone Bridge Crossing the Antietam River

were kept during the bloody day only by their devotion to the South's cause and its leaders. Providence had also smiled upon McClellan by showing to him the battle plans of Lee. A written order setting forth Lee's line of march was picked up by a Union soldier in D.H. Hill's deserted camp and taken to General McClellan, who then knew just where to strike Lee.

On the morning of the nineteenth, a force of Federals crossed the Potomac at Boteler's ford but were met by A.P. Hill's division of Jackson's corps and driven back into the river with great loss. On the northern side of the river, seventy large cannons were planted, raining grape shot upon the Southern men; nevertheless, these

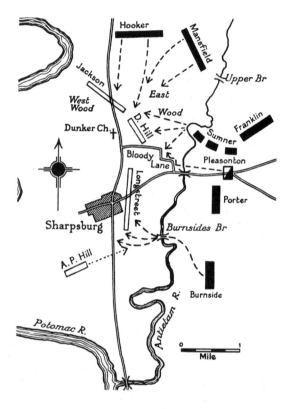

devoted men rushed forward and hurled hundreds of the Federals into the water and then picked them off with steady aim.

While this was happening, a messenger from General Lee found Jackson watching the progress of the fight. His only remark was, "With the blessing of Providence they will soon be driven back." McClellan made no further attempt to follow Lee.

For some weeks, Lee's army lay quietly resting in the lower valley. Jackson, however, was never idle. He was now busy getting clothes and shoes for his men and filling up the ranks which had been severely thinned during the summer. His regiments were then filled up by the return of the sick and the footsore and by new recruits.

Jackson had now become the respected leader of his men. Their pet name for him was "Old Jack." Whenever he rode by, they would cheer themselves hoarse; likewise, his devotion to them was just as great. This story of him is told by an eye witness of the scene:

> When Jackson's men were on their famous march to Manassas at the close of the first day, they found Jackson, who had ridden forward and dismounted, standing upon a great stone by the roadside. His sun burned cap was lifted from his brow and his blue eyes gleamed in the rays of the setting sun. His men burst forth into cheers but he immediately sent an officer to request that there be no cheering, as it might betray their presence to the enemy. Instantly the cheering stopped but as they passed their General their eyes told what their lips could not utter—their love for him. Jackson turned to his staff, his face beaming with delight, and said, 'Who could not conquer with such troops as these?'

Old Jack had every right to be proud of these men who had been marching and fighting for five days. Though many of them having no rations and living upon green corn found along the way, they still had courage and devotion which knew no bounds!

Effects of a 32–pound Shell

Chapter 9

A Lieutenant General

1862-1863

On October 11, 1862, while our hero was in the lower valley, the Confederate government bestowed upon him the rank of lieutenant general. This rank was next to the highest grade in the service. General Lee's army was now divided into two great corps, one of which was given to Jackson, the other to Longstreet. These generals have been called the "two hands" of Lee.

On the eighteenth of October, General Jackson's corps was sent forward to

General James Longstreet

destroy the Baltimore and Ohio railroad. This they did in the most complete way. Burning all the bridges and ripping up the crossties, they finished their work by setting fire to the ties and throwing the iron rails upon the heaps of blazing logs.

After the work was done, Jackson rode over the whole distance, some thirty miles, to see that the destruction was complete.

Towards the end of October, Jackson moved his corps near the Blue Ridge Mountains to watch the movements of McClellan, who was again crossing the Potomac with a vast army of one hundred and forty thousand men.

McClellan's movements, however, were so slow that he was removed from his command and General Burnside was put in his place. As we shall soon see, it was a significant mistake to dismiss George McClellan from command of the Army of the Potomac.

General Burnside resolved to try a new way to Richmond and moved his army towards Fredericksburg on the Rappahannock River. At once, General Lee marched to that town to meet him.

General Ambrose E. Burnside

General Jackson was called from the valley to help Lee and reached General Lee's camp on the first of December. The Southern army numbered altogether about sixty-five thousand men.

General Lee, with two corps, was now upon the heights south of the Rappahannock River while General Burnside, with five corps, held Stafford Heights north of that river. The town of Fredericksburg was between the two armies. The winter set in early and both armies suffered greatly from the cold. The Confederates were for the most part barefooted, without tents and warm clothes, and had only rations of fat meat and corn bread. These trials, however, did not lessen their valor. They dug out trenches, threw up breastworks,[7] and waited for the advance of the enemy.

On the tenth of December, General Burnside began to move his men over the river on pontoon bridges. One hundred and fifty big

---

7.   Hastily-constructed defensive walls (usually breast high) used to protect gunners.

guns on Stafford Heights poured shot and shell upon the town of Fredericksburg, setting it on fire and causing many of the people to leave their homes. By the morning of the thirteenth, ninety thousand Union soldiers had crossed the river. Longstreet held the Confederate left while Jackson held the right.

The battle began by a fierce attack upon Jackson's right which was bravely met; his men fought fiercely, driving the Federals back to the cover of their big guns. At 11:00 A.M., the Federals assaulted Longstreet's position. Again and again, however, they were driven back by the Confederates who did not fire until the foe was close upon them. Charge after charge was made by the Federals but to no avail, for the grim Confederates held their own.

When night came, thirteen thousand Federals lay dead or wounded upon the frozen plain while the Confederates had lost five thousand brave men.

At this time, Jackson ordered a night attack upon Burnside's beaten army, hoping to turn a defeat into a rout and to drive them pell-mell into the river as he had done at Boteler's Ford. His better judgment, however, told him that it was unwise to send his men against the strong works along the river road under the fierce fire of the cannons on Stafford Heights.

So he recalled the order and lost the chance of a decisive victory; for Burnside did not offer battle again but, on the night of the sixteenth, in the midst of a great storm of wind and rain, withdrew his forces to their post on Stafford Heights.

Both armies now went into winter quarters. Jackson's corps built huts in the forests and made themselves as comfortable as possible while their General accepted for his lodgings a cottage at Moss Neck, the home of Mr. Corbin.

Here he set to work to write out reports to the government of his wonderful battles. This he did with great clearness and regard for the truth, recording briefly the exploits of his little army.

Never had a general a more glorious story to tell!

Since the Battle of Kernstown, in March, these brave men had fought the big battles of McDowell, Cross Keys, Port Republic, Cold Harbor, Malvern Hill, Cedar Run, Manassas, Harpers Ferry, Antietam, and Fredericksburg—marched hundreds of miles and captured thousands of prisoners. Never had they quit in battle. When ammunition had given out they fought with stones and, when there had been no food, they lived on roots and berries. So rapidly did they march from place to place that they were called the "foot cavalry" and the knowledge that Jackson was "lost," cast terror into the ranks of the foe. Even their best generals could not tell where Jackson would next be found.

"During the Battle of Cold Harbor," relates one of Jackson's men, "as we were taking back some prisoners, one of them said: 'You think that you are doing great things here but I tell you we are whipping "Old Jack" in the Valley like smoke.' 'Well, maybe you are,' said I, 'because "Old Jack" is here. You've been fighting his men all day.'"

Just then, Jackson rode by with his staff. "There's our General," said I; "now, how much are you whipping us in the Valley?" The man looked dazed and said, "Well, my stars, if that is not 'Old Jack!'"

Indeed, the daring acts of Jackson had made him famous. Not only his own people but strangers from Europe made visits to the camp to see the great general and his men.

During these months of rest, Jackson enjoyed greatly the visits of General Stuart who made the brief period merry with his jokes and cheerful laughter. He also made the acquaintance of little six-year-old Jane Corbin who lived nearby in the big house.

Every evening when the work of the day was over, she would run across to see the General who would always have some little present for her. One evening, having no other gift for her, he ripped off the

General Jackson Crowning Jane Corbin

one band of gold braid from around his new cap and placed it upon her sunny brow.

This lovely child lived only a few months after that. The very day on which General Jackson left Moss Neck in the spring, little Jane was seized with scarlet fever and died after being ill only one day. General Jackson mourned greatly for this little friend. About the same time he heard of the illness of his own baby daughter whom he had never seen.

He had never taken a break since leaving Lexington and, in April, since he could not visit his dear ones, they came to him. He found a quiet home for his wife nearby and great was his pleasure in nursing and caressing his little daughter. He gave her his mother's name—Julia.

During the winter, at Moss Neck, the spiritual development of General Jackson seemed to steadily increase. His chief thought was to live for the glory of God. He often worshiped with his men in the log church which they had built in the forest and toiled early and late for their welfare.

Cooke, the historian, tells us that one day while talking with a member of his staff about the battle which he knew would soon take place, he said: "My trust is in God." A brief silence followed these words and then, rising to his feet, he exclaimed with flashing eyes, "I wish they would come."

The spirit of battle was upon him and he longed to go forward to the fight, which proved to be the last but not least of his wonderful exploits.

General Burnside had been removed from command of the Union army after the Battle of Fredericksburg and General "Fighting Joe" Hooker was put in his place. His army now numbered about one hundred and fifty thousand men.

General Lee's army, to the number of forty-five thousand men, lay entrenched upon the southern banks of the Rappahannock River. General Longstreet's corps was now absent in Suffolk County, therefore, Lee only had one-third as many men as Hooker.

Hooker's plan was to divide his army into two parts. The smaller part was to cross the river near Fredericksburg and engage the Confederates in battle while the larger part would march up the northern bank of the Rappahannock River and, crossing over, reach the flank of Lee's army which would have the foe in front and in the rear. Hooker then planned to send a large troop of cavalry to reach and destroy the railroads leading to Richmond, cutting General Lee off from the capital.

General Joseph Hooker

This was a bold plan but one that was easily guessed by such soldiers as Lee, Jackson, and Stuart. The last named kept watch and, when a movement was made, reported it to Lee. Lee at once fell back to Chancellorsville but not until the main army under General Hooker himself had reached "The Wilderness" beyond Chancellorsville and thrown up strong earthworks. The left wing of Hooker's army under General Sedgwick crossed the river below Fredericksburg on April 29, 1863, and was at once met by Jackson who was always watchful. Sedgwick, however, did not intend to fight but merely to keep General Lee at Fredericksburg while Hooker was gaining the point on Lee's flank. General Lee promptly guessed the plan and ordered General Jackson to leave only one division in front of Sedgwick to proceed at once in search of Hooker and to attack and repulse him. This order reached Jackson about 8:00 P.M. and by midnight his troops were on the march.

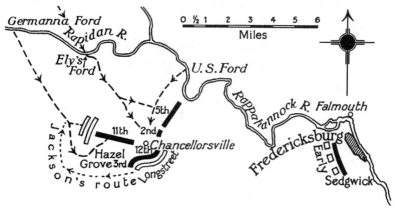

Battle of Chancellorsville

Early the next day, they reached the battlefield where the troops of General Anderson were already engaged with the enemy.

Jackson halted his column and, sending four brigades to the support of Anderson, drew up the remainder of the corps in line of battle upon a ridge near by. The battle raged fiercely all day and, when night came, the Confederates had reached Hooker's first line of entrenchments in the midst of the dense forest.

Meanwhile, General Lee came up with the remainder of the army and a sharp fight took place in front of Hooker's right wing. Night put an end to the contest when, weary and worn, both armies lay down to rest upon the battlefield.

When Lee and Jackson met that night, they were joined by General Stuart who told them that, even though General Hooker had strongly fortified his position upon the east, south, and southwest, he had left the north and west open. Jackson's quick mind at once planned to attack Hooker in the rear just as Hooker had planned to attack Lee.

To the northwest, there were no earthworks and if Jackson could surprise the Federals he would be almost sure of victory. Stuart was there with his gallant horsemen to cover this movement and the

General Robert E. Lee

forests were so dense that Jackson was sure of leading his men silently to the rear of Hooker.

General Lee listened to his arguments and finally gave consent for his great lieutenant to try his plan. General Lee would remain with two divisions in front to engage Hooker while Jackson would march around and strike him in the rear.

By the aid of his chaplain, Rev. Lacy, who knew that country well, General Jackson found a road which would lead him to the rear of Hooker's army. By sunrise he was in the saddle at the head of his column. General Stuart was there to cover his line of march and his troops, knowing at once that their General was making one of his famous flank movements, went forward at a rapid pace. We are told by Dr. McGuire, who was with Jackson, that on the march they were met by General Fitz. Lee told Jackson that Fitz would show him the whole of Hooker's army if he would go to the top of a hill nearby. They went together and Jackson carefully viewed through his glasses the Federal command. He was so wrapped up in his plans that on his return he forgot to salute or thank Fitz. Jackson quickly went back to his army where he ordered one of his aides to go forward and tell General Rodes to cross the plank road and go straight on to the turnpike. He told another aide to go to the rear of the column and see that it was kept closed up. All along the line he kept saying, "Press on, press right on." The strangest energy seemed to possess him.

When he arrived at the plank road he sent this, his last, message to Lee:

> The enemy has made a stand at Chancellorsville. I hope as soon as possible to attack. I trust that an ever kind Providence will bless us with success.

At 3:00 P.M., having marched fifteen miles, he had reached the old turnpike and was exactly on the opposite side of the enemy to that held by General Lee.

He had left the Stonewall Brigade under General Paxton on the plank road with orders to block the way to Germanna Fort. He found the outposts held by Stuart's vigilant troopers who had guarded well his advance. As soon as possible he formed his army in three lines—the division of Rodes in front, that of Colston next, and A. P. Hill's in the rear. Between five and six o'clock in the evening, the word was given and the lines marched forward into the forest.

The thickets were so dense that many soldiers had clothes torn from their backs but on they went, sometimes creeping to get through the thick undergrowth. After a march of two miles, they came suddenly upon the right wing of Hooker's army. The men were scattered about, cooking and eat-

Jackson Leading the Attack

ing their suppers, wholly unconscious of the approach of the dreaded Jackson. With a wild yell, the Confederates dashed forward and drove the enemy pell-mell through the forests for three miles. Jackson's only order was "Press forward" and onward rushed his devoted men after the terrified fugitives.

At 8:00 P.M., the line of General Rodes was within a mile of Chancellorsville but still in the forest. At once, General Jackson ordered the fresh troops of A. P. Hill to advance to the front to relieve those of Rodes who were worn out with marching and fighting.

He knew that Hooker would send forward other troops, therefore, he went to the front himself to get his men in order. As he rode along the line he would say, "Men, get into line! Get into line!" Turning to Colonel Cobb, he said, "Tell General Rodes to take possession of the barricade in front," and then rode away towards the turnpike.

Before the broken ranks of Rodes could gain the barricade, though, Hooker sent forward a large body of fresh troops and the battle was renewed all along the line.

It was now ten o'clock at night and the pale moon sent her silvery rays down into the heart of the dismal wilderness, whose echoes awoke to the sound of tramping feet, the rattle of guns, and the groans of the dying. Through moonlight and shadow, with these sounds ringing in his ears, Jackson rode forward to his death.

Jackson Wounded by His Own Pickets

After riding up the turnpike a short distance, he found the enemy advancing. Turning, he rode back rapidly towards his own line. The Southern men lying hid in the thickets, thinking that Jackson and his staff were a squad of Northern cavalry, opened a rapid fire upon them. So deadly was their aim that nearly every horse in the party was killed. Two officers were killed, others hurt, and General Jackson himself was badly wounded. His left arm was broken just below the shoulder joint and he was also wounded in his lower body. A third ball had entered the palm of his right hand and broke two bones.

His left hand, cruelly hurt, dropped by his side and his horse, no longer controlled by the reins, ran back towards the enemy.

As the horse galloped between two trees, Jackson passed beneath a low branch which struck him in the face, tore off his cap, and threw him violently back in the saddle. He did not fall but grasped the reins with his bleeding right hand and turned back into the road. There, the General found the greatest confusion. Horses, filled with pain and fright, were running in every direction and in the road lay the wounded and dying.

Captain Wilbourne, one of Jackson's aides, now seized the reins and stopped his horse. Seeing that the General was badly hurt, he lifted him from the saddle. He was then laid down by the side of the road, his head resting upon Captain Wilbourne's breast while a messenger went to summon Dr. McGuire, his chief surgeon. Soon General Hill came up and, pulling off the General's gauntlets,[8] found that his left arm was broken and bleeding badly.

As the enemy were not far off, his arm was quickly bandaged with a handkerchief and he tried to walk. After they had gone a few steps, however, a stretcher was brought and the General was placed upon it.

The stretcher was hardly in motion when the fire from the guns of the enemy became terrible. Many men were struck down by it, among whom were General Hill and one of the men who carried the stretcher.

The stretcher was placed upon the ground and the officers lay down by it to escape death.

After awhile the fire changed and Jackson rose to his feet and walked slowly on, leaning upon two members of his staff. General Pender, coming up, saw by the moonlight that General Jackson was badly hurt. "Ah! General," said he, "I am sorry to see that you have

---

8.   Long gloves with flaring cuffs covering the lower part of the arms.

General Jackson's Last Order:
"You must hold your ground, General Pender!
You must hold your ground!"

been wounded. The lines here are so much broken that I fear we will have to fall back."

Though almost fainting, Jackson raised his head and said: "You must hold your ground, General Pender! You must hold your ground!" This was the last order of Jackson on the field.

The General, being very faint, was again placed on the stretcher and the whole party moved through the forest towards the hospital at Wilderness Run.

As they were going slowly through the undergrowth, one of the men caught his foot in a grapevine and fell, letting the stretcher fall to the ground.

Jackson fell upon his wounded shoulder and, for the first time, groaned most piteously. With great difficulty, they made their way until they came to a place in the road where an ambulance was waiting. The General was placed in it and was soon met by his surgeon, Dr. McGuire, who, having sprung into the ambulance, found the General almost without a pulse.

Some liquids were given to him which revived him and after a short time he was laid tenderly in a camp bed at the hospital. Here he fell into a deep sleep. About midnight he was awakened and told by Dr. McGuire that it was thought best to amputate his arm.

"Do what you think best, Doctor," was the calm reply.

The arm was amputated and the ball taken out of his right hand by the skillful surgeon. Once again, he fell into a quiet sleep which lasted until nine o'clock on Sunday morning.

General Hill being wounded, General Stuart was placed in command of Jackson's corps. He now determined to wait until morning to attack the strong works of Hooker which were again in front of the Confederates.

The next morning Stuart thundered on the west and Lee on the east and south. When the Stonewall Brigade went forward, they shouted, "Charge, and remember Jackson!" "But even as they moved from their position," says Dr. Dabney, "General Paxton, the friend and former adjutant of Jackson, was killed where he stood. His men, however, rushed forward and, without any other leader than the name which formed their battle cry, swept everything before them." At 10:00 A.M., May 3, Chancellorsville was taken by Lee and the Federals took refuge behind new barricades closer to the river.

Meanwhile, General Sedgwick, who had been left at Fredericksburg by General Hooker, attacked General Early and captured a part of his command. General Lee, having Hooker in check, sent help to Early and, on Wednesday, came up himself and drove General Sedgwick back across the river where Hooker had already retreated on Tuesday night, May 5.

When General Jackson awoke on Sunday morning, May 3, he asked one of his aides to go to Richmond for his wife. He had sent her to that city when the Federals had begun to move across the river. His mind was clear and he stated that if he had another hour of daylight, he would have cut off the enemy from the field of battle and they would have been obliged either to fight their way out or to surrender.

It was now thought best to take him to a more quiet place. On Monday, he was moved to Mr. Chandler's near Guinea's Depot where every care was taken to make him comfortable. He seemed to take much interest in hearing of the battle on Sunday and said of the Stonewall Brigade, "They are a noble body of men. The men who live through this war will be proud to say: 'I was one of the Stonewall Brigade.'"

He then continued to say that the name of Stonewall belonged to the men of the Brigade alone, as they had earned it by their steadfast conduct at First Manassas. He spoke also of General Rodes and said that, because of gallant conduct, he deserved to be advanced to the rank of major general.

The death of General Paxton gave him great distress but he grew calmer when he heard of the glorious exploits of his old brigade.

He was very pleased to receive a noble letter from General Lee:

General:

I have just received your note, informing me that you were wounded. I cannot express my regret at the occurrence. Could I have directed events; I should have chosen, for the good of the country, to have been disabled in your stead.

I congratulate you upon the victory at Chancellorsville which is due to your skill and energy.

Most truly yours,

R. E. Lee, General

On Wednesday, his wounds were doing so well that it was thought possible to take him by railroad to Richmond. On that night, however, while Dr. McGuire was absent from him for awhile, he was taken with a severe pain in his side which was caused by pneumonia which had now set in.

From that time he grew weaker and, at last, it was seen that he could live only a few hours. The mind of our brave General seemed to constantly dwell on the love and mercy of his Savior Jesus Christ. He was entirely submissive to the will of Almighty God. He lived out one of his favorite sayings about life as he battled the enemy of death: "Do not take counsel of your fears."

Mrs. Jackson came on Thursday and to her he said, "I know you would gladly give your life for me but I am perfectly resigned." When his weeping wife at last told him that death was near, he whispered, "Very good, very good, it is all right." He then sent messages to many friends and wished to be buried in Lexington in the Valley of Virginia.

His little girl was now brought in to receive his last farewell.

Upon seeing her, his face lit up with a bright smile and he murmured, "Little darling!" He tried to caress her with his poor maimed hand as she smiled with delight at seeing him again. She stood by his side upon the bed until it was seen that he was growing very weak.

Then his mind began to wander and, as though again upon the battlefield, he cried out: "Order A.P. Hill to prepare for action!" "Move the infantry to the front!" "Tell Major Hawks to send forward provisions for the men!" Then his vision changed and he murmured, "Let us cross over the river and rest under the shade of the trees."

Cooke reminisces:

> The moment had indeed come when the great leader was to pass over the dark river, which separates two worlds, and rest under the shade of the Tree of Life. From this time, he continued to sink and, at fifteen minutes past three in the afternoon, on Sunday, the tenth of May [1863], he peacefully expired.

The bloody War Between the States continued to turn in favor of the Union army as the Confederate armies slowly began to dwindle away. Finally in 1865, the commander of the Confederate armies, Robert E. Lee, surrendered his troops to General Grant, the Union commander. The long war left millions of Americans dead on the field of battle.

House Where General Jackson Died

Sadly, many of the important issues that lead to the War Between the States were not settled during the conflict. It would take the American people many years to work out their major differences in such areas as State's rights and economic policies. Thankfully, the war did begin the process of freedom for the Negro slaves. The black slaves would no longer be treated as mere property to be bought and sold. One of the few good results of the War Between the States was that it helped to reestablish the truth that "all men are created equal."

As for the gallant Thomas "Stonewall" Jackson, his memory will live on in the hearts of all Americans as a fine example of a dedicated and courageous Christian warrior.

House Where General Lee Signed the Terms of Surrender

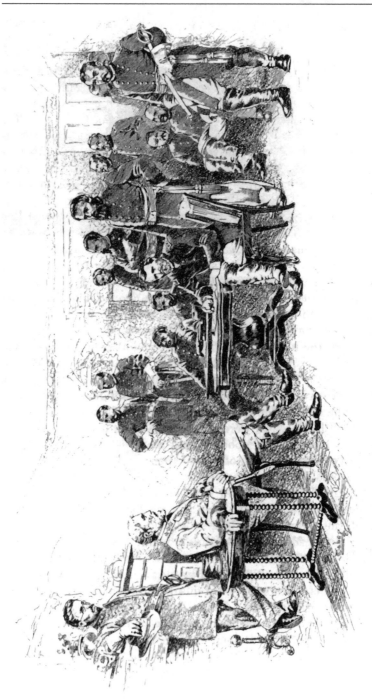

General Lee and General Grant at the end of the War Between the States

Chapter 10

Upon the Roll of Fame

Upon hearing the news of Jackson's death, the grief of the South was equaled only by the wish to do him honor.

President Davis sent a special train to carry his remains to Richmond. He also sent, as the gift of the country, the beautiful new flag of the Confederate Congress to be his winding sheet.[9]

When the train reached Richmond, it was met by a vast concourse of weeping people. On Wednesday, the coffin, which was preceded by military, was carried from the Governor's Mansion to the Capitol through the main streets of the city. The hearse was drawn by four white horses and followed by eight generals as pallbearers. Then came his horse, dressed for battle and led by his personal servant; then followed his staff, the President, the Governor of Virginia, the city authorities, and a vast number of sorrowing people.

As the procession moved along, cannons were fired and bells tolled. Eventually, the Capitol was reached and the body was carried, amid the tears of the multitude, into the building where it lay in state all day. Twenty thousand persons are said to have passed in front of the body to gaze for the last time upon their mighty chief.

It is said that President Davis stood long, gazing at the quiet face, and then in silence left the house. Old soldiers pressed around the coffin with tears streaming down their bronzed faces.

The next day, the remains were carried, attended by a guard of honor, to Lexington where they were received by General Smith, the corps of cadets, the professors, and many sorrowing citizens. Escorted by infantry, cavalry, and artillery, under command of Col. Shipp, Jackson was then carried to the grave by a group from the

---

9. A cloth in which the body of a dead person is wrapped for burial; a shroud.

cadet battery. He was laid to rest beside the graves of his first wife, Elinor Junkin, and child in the beautiful cemetery of Lexington.

The "right hand" of Lee was taken away just as its heaviest stroke had fallen upon the enemy. General Lee, the army, the whole South mourned for their fallen hero. There were other generals as brave and true as Jackson but none who had his keen insight into the movements of the enemy, his love of action, and the wonderful certainty of victory which made him a model to his own soldiers and the dread of the foe.

The fame of Jackson did not remain confined to the limits of his own land. It crossed the ocean and, for decades, the plans of his battles in the Valley of the Shenandoah, of Second Manassas, and of Chancellorsville were studied by military men and used by them as models of strategy and tactics. All English-speaking people are justly proud that the greatest military genius of the nineteenth century belongs to them.

Not long after the end of the war, his admirers and friends in England presented to the State of Virginia a statue of Jackson in bronze. It was placed in the Capitol Square in Richmond not far from the statue of Washington and the great Virginians of his time.

In the spring of 1891, a beautiful and imposing statue of our hero was erected in Lexington, Virginia, by his old soldiers and friends throughout the South. On July 21 of that year, it was unveiled in the presence of a vast multitude of people. This date was the anniversary of the Battle of First Manassas when Jackson, in a "baptism of fire," received the new name of "Stonewall." This anniversary was thought a fitting day to display to his countrymen his figure in enduring bronze.

For days and nights, the trains bore into the historic town crowds of soldiers and visitors from all parts of the country. Beautiful mottoes graced the buildings and highways and the whole event was crowned by perfect weather.

At 12:00 M., the great parade moved from the Virginia Military Institute. General James A. Walker, the only commander of the Stonewall Brigade then living, was chief marshal of the day.

As the procession moved on, band after band of Confederates were seen—battle-scarred veterans in the old Confederate grey, military companies in bright uniforms, famous generals with bronzed faces and grizzled hair, the chaplains of the Confederacy, and visiting camps of veterans from other states.

Following these came the officers of the Virginia Military Institute and Washington and Lee University. Finally, came a large concourse of citizens and carriages. Among those in the carriages were: General Jubal A. Early, the orator of the day, and his host, General Curtis Lee; the sculptor of the statue, Edward V. Valentine; Mrs. General T. J. Jackson and her son-in-law, Mr. Christian, and his children, Julia and Thomas Jackson Christian.

At last, the grandstand in the University grounds was reached. After prayer and the reading of three Confederate war poems— "Stonewall Jackson's Way," "Slain in Battle," and "Over the River," General Early, clad in Confederate grey, made the address which gave a simple account of the great battles fought by Jackson. He was greeted with hearty cheers and tears rolled down the cheeks of many veterans as they again in memory fought and marched with the brave Jackson.

At the end of the speech, the procession again formed and marched to the cemetery where the monument stood.

At the given signal, Mrs. Jackson and her two grandchildren, Julia Jackson Christian, age five years, and Thomas Jackson Christian, age three years, mounted the steps of the platform. A single gun sounded and the two children with united hands pulled the cord and let the veil fall, revealing to admiring thousands the face and form of Jackson.

Cheers and shouts filled the air while the Rockbridge Artillery fired a salute of fifteen guns from the cannons which they had used at Manassas.

The statue, clad in the uniform of a major general, stands with the left hand grasping a sheathed sword, upon which the weight of the body seems to rest. The right hand rests upon the thigh and holds a pair of field glasses which it would seem that the General has just been using.

The figure is eight feet high and stands upon a granite pedestal ten feet tall. Upon the stone are carved only the words, "Jackson, 1824–1863," and "Stonewall."

Under the monument, in a vault, rest the remains of the dead soldier and his daughters Mrs. Julia Christian and Mary Graham who died in infancy.

The veterans lingered long about their beloved hero. Often, had they followed him on the weary march and through the smoke of battle and now it seemed as though he were with them again to lead them on to victory. At last, saluting, they marched in silence away, carrying his image in their memories and the love of him in their hearts.

Not enough, however, had been done to honor our hero. In 1896, a noble building called the "Jackson Memorial Hall" was completed at the Virginia Military Institute and dedicated with fitting ceremony to the memory of Jackson. In these halls and beneath the shadow of this building, the cadets of the South for many long years will be trained for war. How fit the place! Nearby rest Lee and Stonewall Jackson—mighty soldiers and Christian warriors.